D0854736

2 2 AUG 2019

~~?19~~

DIARY OF AN
ORDINARY
SCHOOLGIRL

DIARY OF AN ORDINARY SCHOOLGIRL

MARGARET FORSTER

With an introduction by
Hunter Davies

CHATTO & WINDUS
LONDON

1 3 5 7 9 10 8 6 4 2

Chatto & Windus, an imprint of Vintage,
20 Vauxhall Bridge Road,
London SW1V 2SA

Chatto & Windus is part of the Penguin Random House group of companies
whose addresses can be found at global.penguinrandomhouse.com.

Penguin
Random House
UK

First published by Chatto & Windus in 2017

penguin.co.uk/vintage

A CIP catalogue record for this book is available from the British Library

ISBN 9781784742232

Designed by Anna Green at siulendesign.com

Printed and bound in Great Britain by Clays Ltd, St Ives Plc

INTRODUCTION

My wife Margaret Forster, novelist and biographer, wife and mother, died on 8 February 2016. It was a year before I got round to clearing her writing room. It wasn't superstition, romance, ghoulishness, fear, respect. I just never got round to it. I was so busy. I did tell our two daughters to clear out all her clothes, which they did, a week after the funeral, quite forgetting Margaret had a wonderful pair of Biba boots, purple canvas, laces tied right up to the knee, awfully fashionable in 1965 and now a collector's item. Some lucky Oxfam shop got them.

Then at Christmas I started to go through her desk and files. I found 60 pages of an unfinished novel, marked '27', as it would have been her 27th novel. It was on the top of her desk, so I could hardly miss it. I should have moved it in February after she died, put it in a drawer, as all summer the sun had rained down through her window at the back of the house and the top pages had curled and the ink fast faded. She wrote in ink, all her life.

I eventually put it away safely, then I opened her two top drawers – and found one million words. These were her diaries, which I had never read. They start with three schoolgirl diaries, one when she was eleven in 1949, then at the ages of fourteen and sixteen. From 1973 until not long before she died she wrote a massive diary for a year every five years, filling a whole page every day, all in her immaculate handwriting, each diary coming to about 100,000 words.

They were not a secret. Our children and I knew she kept a diary, but she always dismissed it, saying it was purely family trivia, only about the children, as they were growing up, their funny little ways, not about herself. Now and again over the decades, during our fifty-five years of marriage, if we were arguing about what age Jake could read and write, or when Flora had her first tooth, Margaret would go up to her room and check her diaries. With a bit of luck, the answers would be there.

Slowly I began flicking through. I quickly discovered that though the diaries were indeed mainly about the children, as she had always told us, they were more than that. They were also about her struggles trying to fit in her work, observations and thoughts about our relations, neighbours and friends, the world outside, about herself and me.

Her adult diaries begin when Caitlin, our oldest child, was nine, Jake six and Flora just a newborn baby. They had me laughing with tears in my eyes. They brought it all back.

Margaret, in all her novels, did not really do humour, play things for laughs. Her books were almost always about women, their relationships with each other, or with their parents and children, fairly serious, sensitive stuff, though she was very good on dialogue. Sometimes, as in *Have the Men Had Enough?*, a novel about Alzheimer's, the dialogue was witty and amusing. But mostly, when I read the final proof of a new novel, which I was never allowed to do until it was all over, as she did not want to hear my boring opinion, I would say, 'Not many laughs in this one, pet.'

In real life, telling us stuff round the kitchen table, she was always amusing, describing scenes she had observed, conversations she had overheard, even when we knew she was exaggerating, flamming things up, but in her novels she tended to stick to what she was intending to stick to, the unravelling of a character and a relationship, novels which proved remarkably popular in Germany, the USA and in Britain.

So that was the first big surprise in reading her grown-up diaries – laughing aloud. The second was her strong opinions, about other people – summing them up, getting to the heart of them – and with equally strong opinions about the books she was reading.

The third element, running for forty years, through almost all her adult diaries, was cancer, which first struck in 1975. She records the awful black comedy of cancer, but more often the fear, worrying whether it would strike again.

The three schoolgirl diaries are of course totally different, in a different style. I hadn't even known that they existed. So what a surprise. And a delight. The 1954 diary, when she was fifteen/sixteen, is especially illuminating, revealing her emerging personality, her many talents and her cleverness, her strong opinions and fierce ambition. Where did it all come from? Or had it always been there?

*

Margaret was born on 25 May 1938, on the Raffles council estate in Carlisle. Raffles was quite a showcase when it was first erected, before the war, but it soon became a sink estate, one of the worst in the north of England.

Margaret later used her own family background, as described in her schoolgirl diaries, in two of her most popular non-fiction books, *Hidden Lives* (1995), and *Precious Lives* (1998). She agreed to go back to her old house in the 1980s for a *Daily Telegraph* feature about writers going back to their birthplace. The ground-floor windows were boarded up, a woman upstairs was selling drugs from an open window, a beat-up car had been driven through the front hedge and dumped in the front garden which her father Arthur had so lovingly tended throughout her childhood.

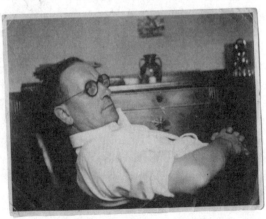

Margaret's father, Arthur Forster, 1900–1996

Arthur Forster, born in 1900, went off on his bike each day in his boiler suit to the local Metal Box factory. He had originally been a motor mechanic then changed to being a fitter, oiling and cleaning the factory machines, working on them when they went wrong.

He did not go in for small talk, disliked social occasions, could be very gruff and abrupt, kept himself to himself. When he took Margaret out as a little girl, if they met any neighbours he would instruct her to 'say nowt'. This was partly the influence of the war – when we were told walls have ears, and the Germans could be listening – but also reflected his personality. He did not want to engage or get mixed up with others. Margaret, in later life, was rather similar. Arthur kept himself to himself, but at the same time he had very strong opinions, things he would do and not do, people and behaviour he disapproved of. He was, however, devoted to his wife Lily.

Her mother Lily, née Hind, 1901–1981

Lily Hind, like Arthur, had left school at thirteen. She could have gone further, if she had had the educational opportunities, but she did secure an office job as a secretary in the council's health department. She had to leave this rather good job the moment she married Arthur in 1931, which was normal for married women at the time.

Their first child was Gordon, born in 1932, so he was six years older than Margaret. On leaving school at fourteen he went to work in Haley's photographic shop and then into the RAF to do his national service. He was a keen Boy Scout, and became a King Scout, the highest honour for any Scout.

Pauline, Margaret's younger sister, was born in 1942, four years after Margaret. She was called Pud or Pudding by Gordon, which wasn't very kind, but the nickname stuck with her for many years, long after it was no longer remotely applicable.

Margaret, right, with sister Pauline and mother

In 1949, when Margaret was eleven, and the first diary begins, she is still living in Raffles, at 144 Orton Road. She and Pauline slept together on a sort of wooden bunk, made by Arthur, in an alcove in a wall, hidden by a curtain. She and Pauline attended the nearest primary school, Ashley Street, one of the more deprived schools in a deprived area, from which very few pupils ever passed the eleven-plus.

The eleven-plus, created after the war, was an examination to be taken by all eleven-year-olds to decide which school they would go to. In Carlisle, the exam was known as the Merit and the top 20 per cent – which was roughly the same proportion throughout the country – went to the Carlisle and County High School for Girls, or to Carlisle Grammar School, which was for boys.

In her 1949 diary, the eleven-plus is therefore hanging over her, but for most of the year her time is taken up with school friends, helping her mother, and the interests of normal ten- and eleven-year-olds, especially eating, and loving sweets. She writes in ink, in neat but rather childish handwriting, in a small Girl Guides Diary. It has sixty printed pages at the beginning on the Girl Guides Promise, plus information about artificial respiration, boating orders, cleanliness, Morse signalling, and what every girl should carry (answer: sharp pencil, small notebook, length of stout cord, small first-aid case, clean handkerchief). She uses the language of the times, picked up from the books she was reading, such as Enid Blyton and schoolgirl stories, so almost everything is 'super' and 'wizard'.

She also records what was in the news, on the radio, in the *Daily Express*, the books she has read, the films she has watched. What was happening in the wider world gets mixed up with doing her homework, helping her mother with the housework, worrying about whether she should get her mop – her hair – cut.

She is ten when the year begins, and in her last year of primary school. On 1 January they go to Grandma's and have 'a lovely tea of salmon'. A week later they go again and have more salmon which this time she says is Grade 1. Tinned of course. Tinned salmon was a great treat. She plays a lot with a boy who lives nearby called Colin Gillespie. He lives in a private semi-detached house, as opposed to Margaret's council house. He is an only child and his mother is very keen on their friendship. Margaret loves going there because Colin's house is nicer, has more space, and his mother supplies lots of art and drawing materials and games for them.

She is not in the Guides, despite having a Guides Diary, but is in the Brownies.

On 23 March 1949 she is furious to learn that Margaret Bell is going up to the Guides. 'Afraid I am rather jealous.'

Two days later, Margaret Bell is still going on about it. 'Margaret Bell Swanked.'

Polyfoto of Margaret aged twelve, in her first year at the Carlisle & County High School for Girls

She gets dressed for Easter, as most Northern girls did at that time, and lists her new clothes. She has a medical check at school and her best friend Doreen tells her that she has heard the doctor say after examining Margaret that Margaret 'is a fine girlie'.

On 20 February, *Down Your Way*, a very popular BBC radio show, comes to Carlisle and a girl she knows, Marion Gosling, is on it. And probably swanking.

On 2 March she writes in large capitals: 'MERIT! MERIT! MERIT! MERIT! MERIT! MERIT! Hope I have PASSED!'

On 13 June she writes: 'Everybody on pins, results come out any morning.'

Next day, she writes: 'Not this time.'

Then the next day: 'Or this time.'

But on Thursday 16 June, the results do arrive. 'HIGH SCHOOL HURRAH.' The next day she adds that Colin, her friend nearby, has passed for the Grammar School.

After this, from July onwards, the 1949 diary entries get thinner. Often she simply writes 'USUAL'. Perhaps the excitement of getting ready to go to the High School was taking up all her time and interest.

School photo – Margaret to the right, behind the man at the front

In 1952 she used a larger-format book, an exercise book, not a printed diary, so she had to write in the month and date herself, usually just writing the date when she began a new week. She is thirteen, and in her third year at the High School.

On the inside front page of the diary, and at the back, she again has a list of all the books she has read that year. The average, she works out, is fifteen per month. At the end of the year she tots up that she has read 136 books. A huge amount, considering how busy she is during the year – not just with schoolwork but swimming, getting up early to go to the baths and train. Her speciality is breaststroke, not speed but style. It never left her, her immaculate, classy, regimented breaststroke.

Another early morning session at the baths for Margaret, right

She is also obsessed by gym work, which surprised me. Throughout 1952 she is endlessly saying how super gym is, how good she is at it. And also playing hockey and tennis. That was all new to me. She never played any games in all the years I knew her – which began properly from the age of eighteen. I wonder what made her give up? Too many other things? Deciding she was an intellectual, not a sportswoman?

During 1952, she is beginning to express more opinions, becoming more assertive, but still very much of her times – so young, innocent, fresh, no boyfriends, no interest in boys or pop culture, apart from reading *Woman* magazine and *Girl*. About the only traditional teenage activity is that she is beginning to sleep in till 11.30 at weekends. It seems light years between her life and interests and activities in 1952 and the life of an average girl of fourteen today.

She is concentrating on her school studies, obsessed by exams and her marks and where she is in the class, and is constantly reading books. But she is also involved in healthy, sporty activities like gym, swimming, walking and cycling. Her new best friend, in her class, is also called Margaret, Margaret Crosthwaite, and they have some super times together. This Margaret has a more middle-class background, her father works in an auctioneers, they own their own house and have holidays in Scotland.

There is still rationing in 1952. But there are excitements, too, such as: 'Great Scandal! Ann Hodgkinson got letter from French penpal, first one. It had vile drawings etc on the back and her father came down to school!!!' When she is really really bored, she either cleans her bike or tidies her school bag …

THE DAY I ENJOYED MOST WAS SATURDAY 16TH MAY 1952
M, my best friend and I set off on our bikes and cycled up to Croglin [village to the east

of Carlisle, on the Pennine slopes] with great laughter and contentment and drinks and rests. Then we went onto the fells. What bliss in the bracken, smiling at the primroses and violets, feeling the glorious warmth of the sun gradually deepening our already lovely tan. Then to roll over and splash in a gurgling pool at the bottom of a stream. See how my writing gets worse and spelling deplorable as my heart races to recall such a day! Then sit on our bikes and swoop down the hills wildly clutching bluebells and yelling at each other, flying through villages amongst the hills, panting and groaning at each other. We were in such happy spirits – oh it was THE MOST PERFECT DAY IN MY LIFE!

So ends her 1952 diary, aged fourteen.

I first heard about Margaret a year before that diary, when she was thirteen and I was fifteen. In 1951, Carlisle United were to play Arsenal in the replay of a Cup game at Brunton Park, Carlisle, which was and is near all the local secondary schools. There were no floodlights in those days so the match was arranged for a Thursday afternoon. All the nearby schools were given the afternoon off, to avoid the crowds.

At my boys' school, we were dancing in the street at the good news. Over at the girls' High School, we heard that a girl was getting up a petition against the half-day holiday. She led a deputation to the head saying that school was much more important than any silly football match, so the half day should be cancelled. We could not believe it. Fortunately her protests failed.

I first met her in the flesh when she was fifteen and I was seventeen. I asked her to dance at a sixth-form youth club. 'I hate dancing,' she said. 'I didn't ask you that,' I said. But she was off.

By then I knew she was a star at her school, the lead in all the school plays, younger girls even asking her for her autograph – and keeping it all their lives. In a small provincial town, in a remote part of the country, with few people in the local sixth forms, and even fewer going on to university – just 4 per cent went in 1954 – she was already standing out, known about even by those who had never met her.

I first went out with her properly in 1956. I was by then at Durham, aged twenty, and she had just turned eighteen. One evening in June or possibly July 1956, while home in Carlisle for the vacation, I happened to be passing the City Picture House, where as always there was an enormous queue. I noticed at the top of the queue was Margaret and her best friend Margaret Crosthwaite, whom I also knew, and two boys who were close friends of mine.

I barged into the queue, pretending they had kept my place, and sat behind them in the cinema, making silly comments about the film. I did not know if they were a foursome, i.e. two couples, but afterwards, on the pavement outside, I realised each was going home alone. So I found myself asking Margaret if I could take her home. I had been rebuffed twice in the previous year or so, but this time, to my amazement, she said yes.

I did not know where she lived, or anything about her family, so I was quite surprised and pleased to discover that she lived on a similar council estate to mine, only at the other end of the town.

What I had not known that evening was that she was demob happy. She had just finished sitting her A levels. For once her mind not filled with schoolwork, hence she had weakened and agreed I could walk her home.

We talked all the way to her house – and that was it. Our non-stop conversation lasted for the next sixty years.

Reading her 1954 diary, which of course I had never read before, I can see so many elements and traits which were in her character when I first met her, but of course it is still an adolescent, juvenile diary, before she has been out into the world beyond Carlisle, her family and school. It is a period piece, about a girl in that particular place at that post-war time. As much as it is Margaret's diary, it is also a piece of social history, so it is being reproduced here in full, with as little as possible in the way of footnotes and explanatory annotations to interfere with the pleasure of reading it. Almost all of it is clear and understandable, even for those who did not have the privilege of being at school in Carlisle in the fifties. Even so, there are a few things that need to be explained here.

By 1954, Margaret's family had moved from the Raffles to a slightly better council estate at Longsowerby, to 180 Richardson Street, dead opposite Carlisle Cemetery. Here, she and Pauline had their own bedroom, but they still shared a bed. This is where she was living when we first started courting in 1956.

180 Richardson Street, Margaret's home in 1954

She is fifteen when the year and the diary begin, but would turn sixteen in May. The big event hanging over her is the exam all grammar school children sat in 1954 at sixteen – and also some secondary-modern children, though that was less common. In her diary she refers to the exam as the School Cert, which was what the exam used to be called, and still was by many teachers and pupils, but technically it had become the General Certificate of Education at O Level. To pass the old School Certificate, you had to pass all six subjects, including maths and English. With O levels, the ones Margaret was about to sit, you were given a pass or fail in each of possibly eight or nine subjects.

Margaret, left, with best friend Margaret Crosthwaite, right

Throughout the year, despite all her schoolwork for the exams, she was constantly reading books, listing and grading each one. She was listening to the radio as well, enjoying the comedy show *Take It From Here*, which most of the nation listened to, and *Paul Temple*, which was considered a rather classy drama detective series, and *Top of the Form*, which was a general knowledge quiz between different schools around the country.

She was also keen on the cinema, as most people were in the fifties. Carlisle had ten cinemas at the time, the two biggest and most popular being the Lonsdale and the City. She was also passionate about plays, which she experienced in two forms.

Plays are a big part of the 1954 diary, but it is not always quite clear what sort of play Margaret is commenting on. There were plays on the radio, most notably the BBC Home Service's *Saturday Night Theatre*, the highlight of the week for many listeners, though during the week other plays were broadcast as well. Very often her Saturday-night treat was ruined by her father coming home from the local pub, the Horse and Farrier. He only went there for a drink once a week on a Saturday evening, but on his return insisted on instantly switching off the radio, or 'knocking it off' as Margaret described it. So, very often, she never heard the end of a good play. There was just one radio set in the house, so everyone had to listen to the same programme.

But she also went to see plays live, at the local theatre. Carlisle, like so many provincial cities, even the smaller ones, had a long-established and handsome theatre, Her Majesty's, where many stars had performed, such as Charlie Chaplin. Her Majesty's was home to a repertory company for several months each summer, usually until the autumn. During this period it was the Salisbury Arts Theatre that came and delighted all vaguely cultured folks in Carlisle of all ages and classes, who would loyally go each week. I used to go with my mother, sitting miles high in the gods, just as Margaret did with her mother.

Margaret's sister Pauline is still being referred to as Pud, or sometimes Pal or Paul. Her brother Gordon is doing his national service in the RAF and has a girlfriend, Shirley, who often comes to the house.

Her best friend at school is still Margaret Crosthwaite, but she has several other close friends, such as Lorna and Doreen. Individuals referred to as Miss are presumably teachers. Gill or Gillian is her pen friend from Liverpool. Gill seems more advanced than Margaret, interested in boys, the soppy thing, and wearing nylons, ugh. The headmistress of the school is Miss Cottrell. Other teachers include Miss Wynne. Jean is a young mother who was very fond of Margaret. Colin is her friend from when they lived in the Raffles. Joan is a friend of Pauline's.

Various aunts come to visit, all called by the initial 'A', for Aunty. Her mother had two sisters, Aunty Nan (AN or Aunty N for short) who has a son called Michael, and Aunty Jean (AJ or Aunty J) who has two boys, the Wallace brothers. Other female relatives are also called Aunty, including Aunty Florrie, a cousin of her mother's, and Aunty Laura.

At school, she is very keen to do well in the annual Rawnsley competition for public speaking. This was named after Canon Rawnsley of Keswick, a great figure in Victorian England, who was a friend and early supporter of Beatrix Potter and became co-founder of the National Trust.

As in the earlier diaries, Margaret mixes national events up with her ordinary home life and school activities. She seems particularly keen on aeroplane crashes, such as the Comet crash of 10 January 1954 when a BOAC de Havilland Comet came down in the sea after leaving Rome, killing all thirty-five people on board. Her interest is fuelled by the extensive coverage of such stories in the *Daily Express* from which she gets a lot of her news and opinions.

Sometimes there are misspellings, which would have been rare for her later in life, but these have been left when they are particularly charming or revealing about her world. There is not a lot of local Carlisle slang, or period slang, apart from 'super' and 'wizard'. 'Rush' – as in 'they'll rush me 1/6 at Thurnams' for a pen nib' – means charge, the inference being that it was extortionate. 'Thick' means unfair. And 'Parliament' was schoolgirl slang code for period. Mop refers to her hair. A Waspie was a tight broad belt, very popular with young girls in the fifties who gave themselves hell by pulling it as tight as possible. 'Pool' means football pools, run by Littlewoods, Vernons and other firms, which were enormously popular in the post-war years, with millions of people, and most dads, placing a modest bet and filling in their coupons predicting the results of the Saturday-afternoon football games.

Silloth played a big part in her young life, as it did for most Carlisle families – a little seaside town on the Solway, about twenty miles away, very handy on the train. During 1954, Margaret's grandmother died, which is how they came to be able to afford a summer holiday in a Silloth guesthouse.

Aged six, on a donkey at Silloth

Many people of a certain age will identify with her life, if not necessarily with her discipline. Despite her humble, non-academic background, she was so keen, so eager, so desperate to study and to learn, the sort of schoolgirl, and schoolboy, who we hope is still with us. They still exist, fired by ambition, though they don't always quite know what it is they want to do, apart from better themselves in some way.

Her 1954 diary is part social history, and part character study. You can see her personality and opinions developing. She herself does not appear aware of this, and would have scoffed at the very suggestion, dismissing such people as soft, but by the end of the year her fellow pupils and some of the teachers do seem to be rather in awe of her. At the age of sixteen, she is showing clear signs of being clever and talented, a young woman with a mind of her own.

Two years after this diary, when Margaret was in the upper sixth, the school encouraged her to try for Oxford and Cambridge. She went to interviews at both, where she met another Margaret – Margaret Drabble – from a Quaker school in York. Our Margaret was accepted by both and decided to go to Oxford. She was awarded an open scholarship to Somerville to read history. Such achievements, coming from a small country grammar school in a remote area, were rare, especially for a girl from her background. Her scholarship made the front page of the *Cumberland News*. Melvyn Bragg, a boy who was at a grammar school ten miles away in Wigton, also got into Oxford

– but the news of his achievement merited less space.

This 1954 diary and Margaret's earlier schoolgirl diaries, for 1949 and 1952, are now in the British Library, along with the manuscripts of all Margaret's books, plus other papers. The later diaries, it is hoped, will join them in due course. It means anyone can go and look at the diaries, if just to admire the handwriting. Goodness, wasn't high school handwriting excellent in those far-off days …

Hunter Davies
London, November 2017

DIARY
1954

CALENDAR 1954

JANUARY
Sunday	...	3	10	17	24	31
Monday	...	4	11	18	25	...
Tuesday	...	5	12	19	26	...
Wednesday	...	6	13	20	27	...
Thursday	...	7	14	21	28	...
Friday	1	8	15	22	29	...
Saturday	2	9	16	23	30	...

FEBRUARY
Sunday	...	7	14	21	28	...
Monday	1	8	15	22	...
Tuesday	2	9	16	23	...
Wednesday	3	10	17	24	...
Thursday	4	11	18	25	...
Friday	5	12	19	26	...
Saturday	6	13	20	27	...

MARCH
Sunday	...	7	14	21	28	...
Monday	1	8	15	22	29	...
Tuesday	2	9	16	23	30	...
Wednesday	3	10	17	24	31	..
Thursday	4	11	18	25	...
Friday	5	12	19	26	...
Saturday	6	13	(20)	27	...

APRIL
Sunday	...	4	11	18	25	...
Monday	...	5	12	19	26	...
Tuesday	...	6	13	20	27	...
Wednesday	...	7	14	21	28	...
Thursday	1	8	15	22	29	...
Friday	2	9	16	23	30	...
Saturday	3	10	17	24	...

MAY
Sunday	...	2	9	16	23	30
Monday	...	3	10	17	24	31
Tuesday	...	4	11	18	(25)	...
Wednesday	...	5	12	19	26	...
Thursday	...	6	13	20	27	...
Friday	...	7	14	21	28	...
Saturday	1	8	15	(22)	29	...

JUNE
Sunday	...	6	13	20	27	...
Monday	...	7	14	21	28	...
Tuesday	1	8	15	22	29	...
Wednesday	2	9	16	23	30	...
Thursday	3	10	17	24	...
Friday	4	11	18	25	...
Saturday	5	12	19	26	...

JULY
Sunday	...	4	11	18	25	...
Monday	...	5	12	19	26	...
Tuesday	...	6	13	20	27	...
Wednesday	...	7	14	21	28	...
Thursday	1	8	15	22	29	...
Friday	2	9	16	23	30	...
Saturday	3	10	17	24	31	...

AUGUST
Sunday	1	8	15	22	29	...
Monday	2	9	16	23	30	...
Tuesday	3	10	17	24	31	...
Wednesday	4	11	18	25	...
Thursday	5	12	19	26	...
Friday	6	13	20	27	...
Saturday	7	14	21	28	...

SEPTEMBER
Sunday	...	5	12	19	26	...
Monday	...	6	13	20	27	...
Tuesday	...	7	(14)	21	28	...
Wednesday	1	8	15	22	29	...
Thursday	2	9	16	23	30	...
Friday	3	10	17	24	...
Saturday	4	11	18	25	...

OCTOBER
Sunday	...	3	10	17	24	31
Monday	...	4	11	18	25	...
Tuesday	...	5	12	19	26	...
Wednesday	...	6	13	20	27	...
Thursday	...	7	14	21	28	...
Friday	1	8	15	22	29	...
Saturday	2	9	16	23	30	...

NOVEMBER
Sunday	...	7	14	21	28	...
Monday	1	8	15	22	29	...
Tuesday	2	9	16	23	30	...
Wednesday	3	10	17	24	...
Thursday	4	11	18	25	...
Friday	5	12	19	26	...
Saturday	6	13	20	27	...

DECEMBER
Sunday	...	5	12	19	26	...
Monday	...	6	13	20	27	...
Tuesday	...	7	14	21	28	...
Wednesday	1	8	15	22	29	...
Thursday	2	9	16	23	30	...
Friday	3	10	17	24	31	...
Saturday	(4)	11	18	25	...

CALENDAR 1955

JANUARY
Sunday	...	2	9	16	23	30
Monday	...	3	10	17	24	31
Tuesday	...	4	11	18	25	...
Wednesday	...	5	12	19	26	...
Thursday	...	6	13	20	27	...
Friday	...	7	14	21	28	...
Saturday	1	8	15	22	29	...

FEBRUARY
Sunday	...	6	13	20	27	...
Monday	...	7	14	21	28	...
Tuesday	1	8	15	22	...
Wednesday	2	9	16	23	...
Thursday	3	10	17	24	...
Friday	4	11	18	25	...
Saturday	5	12	19	26	...

MARCH
Sunday	...	6	13	20	27	...
Monday	...	7	14	21	28	...
Tuesday	1	8	15	22	29	...
Wednesday	2	9	16	23	30	...
Thursday	3	10	17	24	31	...
Friday	4	11	18	25	...
Saturday	5	12	19	26	...

APRIL
Sunday	...	3	10	17	24	...
Monday	...	4	11	18	25	...
Tuesday	...	5	12	19	26	...
Wednesday	...	6	13	20	27	...
Thursday	...	7	14	21	28	...
Friday	1	8	15	22	29	...
Saturday	2	9	16	23	30	...

MAY
Sunday	1	8	15	22	29	...
Monday	2	9	16	23	30	...
Tuesday	3	10	17	24	31	...
Wednesday	4	11	18	25	...
Thursday	5	12	19	26	...
Friday	6	13	20	27	...
Saturday	7	14	21	28	...

JUNE
Sunday	...	5	12	19	26	...
Monday	...	6	13	20	27	...
Tuesday	...	7	14	21	28	...
Wednesday	1	8	15	22	29	...
Thursday	2	9	16	23	30	...
Friday	3	10	17	24	...
Saturday	4	11	18	25	...

JULY
Sunday	...	3	10	17	24	31
Monday	...	4	11	18	25	...
Tuesday	...	5	12	19	26	...
Wednesday	...	6	13	20	27	...
Thursday	...	7	14	21	28	...
Friday	1	8	15	22	29	...
Saturday	2	9	16	23	30	...

AUGUST
Sunday	...	7	14	21	28	...
Monday	1	8	15	22	29	...
Tuesday	2	9	16	23	30	...
Wednesday	3	10	17	24	31	...
Thursday	4	11	18	25	...
Friday	5	12	19	26	...
Saturday	6	13	20	27	...

SEPTEMBER
Sunday	...	4	11	18	25	...
Monday	...	5	12	19	26	...
Tuesday	...	6	13	20	27	...
Wednesday	...	7	14	21	28	...
Thursday	1	8	15	22	29	...
Friday	2	9	16	23	30	...
Saturday	3	10	17	24	...

OCTOBER
Sunday	...	2	9	16	23	30
Monday	...	3	10	17	24	31
Tuesday	...	4	11	18	25	...
Wednesday	...	5	12	19	26	...
Thursday	...	6	13	20	27	...
Friday	...	7	14	21	28	...
Saturday	1	8	15	22	29	...

NOVEMBER
Sunday	...	6	13	20	27	...
Monday	...	7	14	21	28	...
Tuesday	1	8	15	22	29	...
Wednesday	2	9	16	23	30	...
Thursday	3	10	17	24	...
Friday	4	11	18	25	...
Saturday	5	12	19	26	...

DECEMBER
Sunday	...	4	11	18	25	...
Monday	...	5	12	19	26	...
Tuesday	...	6	13	20	27	...
Wednesday	...	7	14	21	28	...
Thursday	1	8	15	22	29	...
Friday	2	9	16	23	30	...
Saturday	3	10	17	24	31	...

CHURCH FESTIVALS

Circumcision	..	January 1
Epiphany	..	" 6
1st Sunday after Epiphany	..	" 10
2nd " " "	..	" 17
3rd " " "	..	" 24
Conversion of St. Paul	..	" 25
4th Sunday after Epiphany	..	" 31
Purification of B.V. Mary	..	February 2
5th Sunday after Epiphany	..	" 7
Septuagesima Sunday	..	" 14
Sexagesima Sunday	..	" 21
St Matthias, Apostle	..	" 24
Quinquagesima Sunday	..	" 28
Ash Wednesday	..	March 3
Quadragesima—1st Sunday in Lent	..	" 7
2nd Sunday in Lent	..	" 14
3rd " " "	..	" 21
Annunciation of B.V. Mary	..	" 25
4th Sunday in Lent	..	" 28
Passion Sunday	..	April 4
Palm Sunday	..	" 11
Good Friday	..	" 16
Easter Day	..	" 18
Low Sunday	..	" 25
St Mark, Evangelist	..	" 25
SS. Philip and James	..	May 1
2nd Sunday after Easter	..	" 2
3rd " " "	..	" 9
4th " " "	..	" 16
Rogation Sunday	..	" 23
Ascension Day (Holy Thursday)	..	" 27
Sunday after Ascension	..	" 30
Whit Sunday	..	June 6
St. Barnabas	..	" 11
Trinity Sunday	..	" 13
1st Sunday after Trinity	..	" 20
St. John, Baptist	..	" 24
2nd Sunday after Trinity	..	" 27
St. Peter, Apostle	..	" 29
3rd Sunday after Trinity	..	July 4
4th " " "	..	" 11
5th " " "	..	" 18
6th " " "	..	" 25
St. James, Apostle	..	" 25
7th Sunday after Trinity	..	August 1
Transfiguration	..	" 6
8th Sunday after Trinity	..	" 8
9th " " "	..	" 15
10th " " "	..	" 22
St. Bartholomew	..	" 24
11th Sunday after Trinity	..	" 29
12th " " "	..	September 5
13th " " "	..	" 12
14th " " "	..	" 19
St. Matthew, Apostle	..	" 21
15th Sunday after Trinity	..	" 26
St. Michael and All Angels	..	" 29
16th Sunday after Trinity	..	October 3
17th " " "	..	" 10
18th " " "	..	" 17
St. Luke, Evangelist	..	" 18
19th Sunday after Trinity	..	" 24
SS. Simon and Jude	..	" 28
20th Sunday after Trinity	..	" 31
All Saints' Day	..	November 1
21st Sunday after Trinity	..	" 7
22nd " " "	..	" 14
Last " " "	..	" 21
Advent Sunday	..	" 28
St. Andrew, Apostle	..	" 30
2nd Sunday in Advent	..	December 5
3rd " " "	..	" 12
4th " " "	..	" 19
St. Thomas, Apostle	..	" 21
Christmas Day	..	" 25
1st Sunday after Christmas	..	" 26
St. Stephen, Martyr	..	" 26
St. John, Evangelist	..	" 27
Holy Innocents	..	" 28

The Astronomical information in this Diary is based on Crown Copyright data supplied by the Nautical Almanac Office and is printed with the permission of the Controller of H.M. Stationery Office.

Greenwich Mean Time is given throughout and allowance must be made for Summer Time.

COMMON NOTES

Golden Number	..	XVII
Epact	..	25
Solar Cycle (Year of)	..	3
Dominical Letter	..	C
Roman Indiction (Year of)	..	7
Julian Period (Year of)	..	6667
Queen's Accession (1952)	..	February 6
Spring begins	..	March 21
Mothering Sunday	..	" 28
Festival of Passover	..	April 18
Primrose Day	..	" 19
Queen Elizabeth II born (1926)	..	" 21
Ramadan (Moslem)	..	May 4
Unconditional Surrender of Germany ratified in Berlin (1945)	..	" 9
Queen Mary born (1867)	..	" 26
Duke of Edinburgh born (1921)	..	June 10
Fathers' Day	..	" 19
Summer begins	..	" 21
St. Swithin's Day	..	July 15
Queen Elizabeth, the Queen Mother, born (1900)	..	August 4
Unconditional Surrender of Japan (1945)	..	" 14
Mohammedan New Year (A.H. 1374)	..	" 30
Great Britain declared war on Germany (1939)	..	September 3
Autumn begins	..	" 23
Jewish New Year (A.M. 5715)	..	" 28
Day of Atonement (Yom Kippur)	..	October 7
Feast of Tabernacles	..	" 12
El Alamein Offensive (1942)	..	" 23
United Nations' Day	..	" 24
Prince Charles, Duke of Cornwall, born (1948)	..	November 14
Great Britain and U.S.A. declared war on Japan (1941)	..	December 8
Winter begins	..	" 22

BANK HOLIDAYS

England, Northern Ireland and Irish Republic

St. Patrick's Day (Ireland only)	..	March 17
Good Friday	..	April 16
Easter Monday	..	April 19
Whit Monday	..	June 7
Orangeman's Day (N. Ireland)	..	July 12
First Monday in August	..	August 2
Christmas Day (Saturday)	..	December 25
Boxing Day	..	December 27

Scotland

New Year's Day (Friday)	..	January 1
Good Friday	..	April 16
First Monday in May	..	May 3
First Monday in August	..	August 2
Christmas Day (Saturday)	..	December 25

QUARTER DAYS

England and Ireland	Scotland	
Lady Day .. Mar. 25	Candlemas .. Feb. 2
Midsummer .. June 24	Whitsunday .. May 15
Michaelmas .. Sept. 29	Lammas .. Aug. 1
Christmas .. Dec. 25	Martinmas .. Nov. 11

LAW SITTINGS | DINING TERMS

Hilary Jan. 11-Apr. 14	Hilary Jan. 20-Feb. 11
Easter Apr. 27-June 4	Easter Apr. 28-May 20
Trinity June 15-July 31	Trinity June 16-July 8
Mclmas Oct. 1-Dec. 21	Mclmas. Nov 3-Nov 25

LAW VACATIONS

Christmas Dec. 24-Jan. 6	Whitsun June 5-June 8
Easter April 16-April 20	Long Aug. 1-Sept. 30

UNIVERSITY TERMS

Oxford Full Terms	Cambridge Full Terms
Hilary Jan. 17-Mar. 13	Lent Jan. 12-Mar. 12
Trinity April 25-June 19	Easter April 20-June 11
Mclmas Oct. 10-Dec. 4	Mclmas. Oct. 5-Dec. 3

SUN'S RISINGS AND SETTINGS

For every **SATURDAY** in 1954
Greenwich Mean Time

	Rises h.m.	Sets h.m.			Rises h.m.	Sets h.m.
JAN. 2	8 6	4 2	JULY 3		3 48	8 20
9	8 4	4 10	10		3 54	8 15
16	7 59	4 21	17		4 1	8 10
23	7 52	4 32	24		4 10	8 2
30	7 43	4 45	31		4 21	7 51
FEB. 6	7 32	4 58	AUG. 7		4 32	7 39
13	7 20	5 10	14		4 42	7 26
20	7 6	5 23	21		4 53	7 12
27	6 51	5 36	28		5 5	6 57
MAR. 6	6 36	5 48	SEPT. 4		5 16	6 41
13	6 21	6 0	11		5 27	6 25
20	6 5	6 12	18		5 38	6 10
27	5 49	6 24	25		5 49	5 54
APR. 3	5 33	6 35	OCT. 2		6 1	5 37
10	5 17	6 47	9		6 12	5 22
17	5 2	6 59	16		6 24	5 7
24	4 47	7 10	23		6 36	4 52
MAY 1	4 34	7 21	30		6 49	4 39
8	4 21	7 33	NOV. 6		7 0	4 26
15	4 9	7 44	13		7 13	4 15
22	3 59	7 54	20		7 25	4 5
29	3 52	8 3	27		7 36	3 58
JUNE 5	3 46	8 10	DEC. 4		7 47	3 53
12	3 43	8 16	11		7 55	3 51
19	3 42	8 20	18		8 1	3 52
26	3 44	8 21	25		8 5	3 55

MOON'S PHASES

Greenwich Mean Time

) First Quarter. O Full Moon.
(Last Quarter. ● New Moon.

Jan. 5	●	2.21 a.m.
12	)	12.22 a.m.
19	O	2.37 a.m.
27	(	3.28 a.m.
Feb. 3	●	3.55 p.m.
10	)	8.29 a.m.
17	O	7.17 p.m.
25	(	11.29 p.m.
Mar. 5	●	3.11 p.m.
11	)	5.51 p.m.
19	O	12.42 p.m.
27	(	4.14 p.m.
Apr. 3	●	12.25 p.m.
10	)	5.05 a.m.
18	O	5.48 a.m.
26	(	4.57 a.m.
May 2	●	8.22 p.m.
9	)	6.17 p.m.
17	O	9.47 p.m.
25	(	1.49 p.m.
June 1	●	4.03 a.m.
8	)	9.13 a.m.
16	O	12.06 p.m.
23	(	7.46 p.m.
30	●	12.26 p.m.

July 8	)	1.33 a.m.
16	O	12.29 a.m.
23	(	12.14 a.m.
29	●	10.20 p.m.
Aug. 6	)	6.50 p.m.
14	O	11.03 a.m.
21	(	4.51 a.m.
28	●	10.21 p.m.
Sept. 5	)	12.28 p.m.
12	O	8.19 p.m.
19	(	11.11 p.m.
27	●	12.50 a.m.
Oct. 5	)	5.31 a.m.
12	O	5.10 a.m.
18	(	8.30 p.m.
26	●	5.47 p.m.
Nov. 3	)	8.55 p.m.
10	O	2.29 p.m.
17	(	9.32 a.m.
25	●	12.30 p.m.
Dec. 3	)	9.56 a.m.
10	O	12.56 a.m.
17	(	2.21 a.m.
25	●	7.33 a.m.

ECLIPSES

In the year 1954 there will be five eclipses, three of the Sun and two of the Moon.

1. An Annular Eclipse of the Sun on January 5th, invisible in Great Britain.
2. A Total Eclipse of the Moon on January 19th, visible in Great Britain.
3. A Total Eclipse of the Sun on June 30th, visible as a partial eclipse in Great Britain.
4. A Partial Eclipse of the Moon on July 15th–16th, visible in Great Britain.
5. An Annular Eclipse of the Sun on December 25th, invisible in Great Britain.

CALENDAR NOTES 1954-57

	1954	1955	1956	1957
January 1st	Friday	Saturday	Sunday	Tuesday
Sundays after Epiphany ...	5	4	3	5
Septuagesima Sunday ...	February 14th	February 6th	January 29th	February 17th
February 1st	Monday	Tuesday	Wednesday	Friday
Ash Wednesday	March 3rd	February 23rd	February 15th	March 6th
March 1st	Monday	Tuesday	Thursday	Friday
April 1st	Thursday	Friday	Sunday	Monday
Palm Sunday	April 11th	April 3rd	March 25th	April 14th
Good Friday	April 16th	April 8th	March 30th	April 19th
Easter Day	April 18th	April 10th	April 1st	April 21st
May 1st	Saturday	Sunday	Tuesday	Wednesday
Ascension Day	May 27th	May 19th	May 10th	May 30th
Whit Sunday	June 6th	May 29th	May 20th	June 9th
Trinity Sunday	June 13th	June 5th	May 27th	June 16th
Sundays after Trinity ...	23	24	26	23
June 1st	Tuesday	Wednesday	Friday	Saturday
July 1st	Thursday	Friday	Sunday	Monday
August 1st	Sunday	Monday	Wednesday	Thursday
August Bank Holiday ...	August 2nd	August 1st	August 6th	August 5th
September 1st	Wednesday	Thursday	Saturday	Sunday
October 1st	Friday	Saturday	Monday	Tuesday
November 1st	Monday	Tuesday	Thursday	Friday
Advent Sunday	November 28th	November 27th	December 2nd	December 1st
December 1st	Wednesday	Thursday	Saturday	Sunday
Christmas Day	Saturday	Sunday	Tuesday	Wednesday
December 31st	Friday	Saturday	Monday	Tuesday

JANUARY
1954

1
FRIDAY
Holiday—Australia, Canada, New Zealand,
Scotland, S. Africa, U.S.A.

Started the Year well I dont think with a grand row with Gordon, the beast. I broke all my resolutions and fled up stairs in a screaming rage and nearly broke the door. So spent a chilly afternoon up their rather than face that ---! Shirley, his girl came up and they started a soppy carry on. Went to the flics with Pud. The newsreel of the Queen was G

2
SATURDAY
Slept in! Disgusting so was in a flaming temper. Did the chores in a vicous mood. Went to town & Mum got a new skirt cardigan. The Newspapers are full of those diplomats that disappeared, Burgess and Maclean. Great controvery over wether in Russia. Bet they are, the blinking traitor England's got to watch Russia & Malenkov, strikes me.

3
SUNDAY
2nd after Christmas

Pud came back from her nativity play with her face like a cox pippin! What a spectacle. Thought she was it, too. Mum said it was quite good, in Pud VG.

4
MONDAY
Duchess of Winsor lost her place as worlds best dressed women today. Bets she's mad! Princess M. was eigth. Got a belated Xmas present from Bill, my pen pal. Soppy chiffon scarf, but very nice hankies. They are showing June frocks in January in the papers. Daft! Had an ordinary washing day, Knowing in afternoon I had plenty to do - but doing nothing. Very nice!

1
FRIDAY

Started the Year well I dont think with a grand row with Gordon, the beast. I broke all my resolutions and fled upstairs in a screaming rage and nearly broke the door. So spent a chilly afternoon up their rather than face that … Shirley, his girl came up and they started a soppy carryon. Went to the flics with Pud. The newsreel of the Queen was G.

2
SATURDAY

Slept in! Disgusting so was in a flaming temper. Did the chores in a vicous mood. Went to town & Mum got a new skirt and cardigan. The Newspapers are full of those diplomats that disappeared, Burgess and Maclean. Great Controversy over wether in Russia. Bet they are, the blinking traitors. Englands got to watch Russia and Malenkov, strikes me.

3
SUNDAY

Pud came back from her nativity play with her face like a cox pippin! What a spectacle. Thought she was it, too. Mum said it was quite good, in fact VG.

4
MONDAY

Duchess of Winsor lost her place as worlds best dressed women today. Bets shes mad! Princess M. was eigth. Got a belated Xmas present from Gill, my pen pal. Soppy chiffon scarf, but very nice hankies. They are showing June frocks in January in the papers. Daft!

Had an ordinary washing day, knowing in afternoon I had plenty to do – but doing nothing. Very nice!

5
TUESDAY

Pud got her hair cut like mine and it looks very nice. It makes her face round instead of oblong. Listened to the last of Mrs Dales Diary I'll get until the Easter holidays. Went to town and got a super Wheatley book from library. But it kept me from French Holiday Verbs! I cant resist them, Im afraid. (the books not the verbs!)

6
WEDNESDAY

Started school again. Good to see all the old mugs again. New secretary. Good face and figure. Old Girl. Miss Haigh started at once nagging "<u>Do</u> be <u>sensible</u>," her warcry. School dinners murder as usual and there were a lot of dirty remarks flying about them! M. and I nearly died in physics at Red Noses antics! We got our experiment right and exchanged gossip with everyone. Everyone howled at my new year resolutions! Miss Wynne very bright and cheery! (!). Got a good seat in form room.

7
THURSDAY

We seem to be getting back into the familiar routine again. Mrs Shaw gave us a French oral for practise for the S.C. It wasn't really very formidable. Recorder class was hilarious as usual and I got Miss Simpson in a screaming rage again. We had some nice easy things to play for once. The eloped senorita and her husband-prospective are having a wonderful time evading Papa Patino!* Giles had a very funny cartoon.†

8
FRIDAY

Just took notes all History all about Metternich in Austrian History. Latin was boring as usual. Double Maths Test in Arithmetic wasn't bad but tussled in vain with one problem. The eloped couple have got married! There were some good pictures of the Queen & the Duke. The flood warnings are going out again. Bitterly cold. Spent a pleasant evening by myself in front of a lovely fire. "Take it from here" was a scream!

9
SATURDAY

Did all the usual chores. Spent the day indoors. Pal got me a book from the library and read it and White Shoes in the evening while the family and Joan played games round the fire. The papers are full of the electricans and engineers proposed strikes. Dad will be in the engineers if it comes off. I think its soft, plain soft. Its just a vicious circle.

10
SUNDAY

The walk over to church was very enjoyable – cold but sunny. I was so nice and warm in my camel coat. The sermon was boring as usual. Wish Mac. was still here.

---

* Runaway Bolivian heiress Isabell Patino had run off with twenty-year-old Old Etonian James Goldsmith.
† In the *Daily Express*, their family newspaper.

11
MONDAY

M. was off so went to see her. She fainted last night and was violently sick, poor thing. But she seemed much better. It was like my other half cut off at school! Had a good chat with her. I love reading the Monday paper with all the fashion news. We got talking about figures at dinner. Jen had 40" hips! I am 34-24-34 & everyone envious! The dinner was okay but not enough of it – not nearly enough!

12
TUESDAY

Everyone is talking of that awful Comet crash yesterday when everyone was killed. The usual tragic stories. Usual Tuesday. Very enjoyable chat in Art! Miss Wynne had an awful Sheridan play – The Critics – lined up for us at the Dramatic Society. We're all trying to think of another play to get away from this dreadful one. M. back at school but had a headache although thats nothing unusual.

13
WEDNESDAY

Smashed my flipping nib in Physics but it still serves, thank goodness. M off this morning, went to see Doctor. She is overaught and overworked as I thought. Miss Fawcett at her ironical best because of bad prep. Cant say I blame her. The play was super tonight. "Night must come" with Richard Burton who was very good as the Welshman. It was a frightfully good murder. Pud was petrified! Miss Haigh was nattery too about bad work! The electrician strike business with that old

Red, Faulkes, is the subject of some howling cartoons, and much controversy. Some delightful pictures of the Queen. She looks so charming.

14
THURSDAY

Another awful plane crash, sabotage know suspected as both took place around Rome. Pretty Foul. Miss Wynne gave us a Macbeth test and talked a lot of twaddle as usual. The Denton Holme Road is up & theirs a fearful mess up. The buses are going all over the place. Its not worth going on my bike so take the bus. Miss Simpson nattery in Recorder. M and I perfected the quickstep double turn.

15
FRIDAY

Algebra maths test not so bad. Very good practice for GCE. Latin dull as usual. I loath old Caesar and his blooming battles. They stink. Mrs A at her wittiest (!) best. The weather was lovely. Howling wind and lashing rain! Pud off with cold. M and I learnt part of the Creep from Doreen. We had a super dancing lesson. Letter from Gill. Usual stuff. Boys, boys and boys! Swiss avalanches are awful. "White" death.

16
SATURDAY

There was terrible damage done by the gales last night. Trees uprooted, houses blown down, TV areials wrenched off. Spent most of the afternoon with Pud who has a bad cold in bed. Learnt a lot of world geography. Know S & N America, Africa and surrounding

countries. So good work done. Also read three schoolgirl books. Lot of rot!

17
SUNDAY

Paulette fractured her wrist and has it in plaster! The
sermon was lousy as per usual but I suppose it doesn't
really count. Perhaps getting a new curate.

18
MONDAY

Had a hair appointment made. My mop sure needs
clipped. The girls going to Paris had a discussion
on clothes to take at dinner and we had great fun.
M enjoyed Ian Reemy's party yesterday with Brian.
I honestly don't know what these soppy fools see in
boys & that isn't sour grapes. There were some super
fashion pictures of nightclothes in todays paper. Quite
Ridiculous but …! Marks had some dresses in.

19
TUESDAY

Dramitic Soc was very good but we could not divert
P Wynne from The Critic by Sheridan in favour of a
modern play! I was casted as Sir Don Ferolo Whisker-
andos because I have a boyish manner and voice! I am
to have lovely brass earrings tights, tunic, cloak and
lovely whiskers! It isn't a very big part but it is one of
the best because its such fun. Wish I could find a sword
that would disappear, it is very effective!

20
WEDNESDAY

Thought we were going to get a film show today – but

it was just LVths. What a sell! So we had to face grim test. Washed my hair after having it cut at Binns. It was like a fuzzy golliwogs. Listened to the play which was very good. "The great Romance" with Robert Morley. Pud still off. Sold biscuits at Recr. for Barnardo effort. We got quite a sum. I, of course, forgot till today and had to go chasing to Liptons for biscuits. They cost me 1/3 out of own money! Broke me. But I suppose it was worth it, we are keeping an orphan after all. Had some lovely fizzy lemonade today and cream cakes.

21
THURSDAY

Stinking old Miss Simpson wouldnt let me off for school council next week. Was <u>furious</u>. Says we've got to practise for the Festival. I'm not going to rotten old recorder if I cant go to S.C. The beast. Shes so horrible. I'm goin to leave if she doesn't let me go. Shes just a frowzy old maid. Stinks. Awful. Shes so selfish. I wouldn't miss school council for worlds. Besides, the form depend on me.

22
FRIDAY

Went to Lonsdale with school to see the Everest film and the Queens tour of Tonga and Fiji. It – they – were terrific! The colours in the Queens Tour were splendid, especially their dresses. The scenery was magnificent – I'd love to go there! The Everest film was too marvellous for words. The snow & ice were wonderful. What they must have gone through! I thought Tenzing was terrific – they all were without exception.

23
SATURDAY

Made a treasure hunt for Pud and Joan this afternoon. Read my European History mostly. Heard half of Saturday Night Theatre, it was very good. Wish it wasn't on so very late. France beat Ireland at Rugger – never thought they would. There were tons of draws today, especially in the 2nd Division North. The 2nd eleven got 14 goals. Phew!

24
SUNDAY

Shirley had a nice new jumper on today. Its like a mad house when we're all in on a Sunday Night! "Take your pick" was very good. Wrote to Gillian.

25
MONDAY

Couldn't make my mind up whether to go to the hym practise or not. Decided not to, even though M & Pat plagued me! Another plane crash today! The girls flying to Paris in the Easter Hols are getting nervy. Hillary goes for her Art interview with the Principal today, do hope she gets in – I'm sure she will though. Shes very good.

26
TUESDAY

Hillary almost definetly in Art school. She is plaguing me to go now. It would mean leaving at the end of this year (gosh Id hate to leave school) taking 4 yrs at Art College & 2 years at University then becoming an Art Mistriss. Yet I've always wanted to be in the 6th & go to University & take a degree. I don't know, I just can't make my mind up. Its awful.

27
WEDNESDAY

Lousy lecture on wool this morning but better than Latin, I suppose. M & I went to see Mr Davidson the Youth Employment officer. He was very helpful & she decided to think about Pharmacy and Archeology. We're going next week when I will ask about Art and History. Very helpful chap. Valerie Hepple won LVL's box of fruit today. Jolly nice. Bitterly cold but otherwise a nice day. Everyone seems to be discussing careers at school. Mary fancies radiography, Pat infant teaching but most of us just haven't a clue. We know what we don't want to do but not what we do want to do. Revised History tonight.

28
THURSDAY

Chased around frantically trying to see Miss S but in vain. So arranged for deputy to go to school council. Was I mad! Then when we arrived at Recorder, a bit late, she asked us why we were late. M muttered "It's a pity we came at all" and she heard, crashed a chord and said "Then you can go!" But would she let me go? Would she dick! Then, to crown it all she said I could have gone to S.C. Oooooooooooo!

29
FRIDAY

We went to the Mass X-ray today. Had a good chat in Art as usual. M is worried about Lorna who is an awful gooseberry. I seem to be the only one able to cure her by sitting on her! Pauline got Tennis shoes so just had to read it! It was very good really – following the tradition of the other "footgear" books. But am not reading any more books till after exams (!).

30
SATURDAY

Worked haard this safternoon at Geog. & History. Finished Revision on them but whether I'll remember them is another matter. Its awful to think its so near! Helped mum in the morning generally. Pud a little nuisance as usual! Never does anything. Listened to Radio tonight, there were some good records on Record Roundabout.

31
SUNDAY

19 children killed yesterday because of thin ice from a freak thaw. 4 brothers were killed. It's a terrible tradegy. The BBC broadcast all day warnings.

FEBRUARY
1954

1
MONDAY

The paper didn't come today, which was most annoying. We got our exam. time table today – looks pretty grim I must say! 5 hours latin & French – I couldn't do it on my Caulida. The school mag. came out today, first time for 15 yrs. It is very interesting – especially the news of the old girls. Some have marvellous careers Started Science revision – loads & loads of it. Ugh!

2
TUESDAY

Had great fun at Dramatic Society today – This play is really great fun to act. To think that this time next week we'll be in the throes of exams! Oh for 3 weeks today! Perfect bliss! Did some physics revision – there seems to be an awful lot. The papers are full of the Germany Conferences between the four powers. Evidently the Russia are getting very tough. Seems a nasty situation.

3
WEDNESDAY

Had a film in physics – good opportunity to gossip! More Science revision. The play was very good tonight it wa "Gaig's Wife" with Phyllis Calvert. All about a selfish domineering wife – everyone deserted her in the end. Carr at school for shaggy dog stories – spent all dinner hour telling them to a crowd of girls. The best one is the indian one. "Indian has very good memory – sees what is going every where. Engiman comes to see him – what had h f breaker on Jan 4th 1928? Indian – eggs. Eng – marvella 20 years later Eng. on business in America. Visits Indian Greets him with "How!" Indian – "fried!" They howled!

[indian] greehng

1
MONDAY

The paper didn't come today, which was most annoying.
We got our exam time table today – looks pretty grim
I must say! 5 hours Latin & French – I couldn't do
½ an hr. Corlida the school mag. came out today, first
time for 15 yrs. It is very interesting – especially the
news of the old girls, some have marvellous careers.
Started Science revision – loads and loads of it. Ugh!

2
TUESDAY

Had great fun at Dramatic Society today. This play is
really great fun to act. To think that this time next week
we'll be in the throes of exams! Oh for 3 weeks today!
Perfect bliss! Did some physics revision – there seems
to be an awful lot. The papers are full of the Germany
Conferences between the four powers. Evedently the
Russians are getting very tough. Seems a nasty situation.

3
WEDNESDAY

Had a film in physics – good opportunity to gossip!
More Science revision. The play was very good tonight
it was "Craigs Wife" with Phyllis Calvert. All about a
selfish domineering wife – everyone deserted her in the
end. Craze at school for shaggy dog stories – spent all
dinner time telling them to a crowd of girls. The best
one is the Indian One. "Indian has very good memory
– sees what is going on everywhere. Eng'man comes
to see him – what had I for breaker on Jan 4th 1928?
Indian – eggs. Eng – marvellous. 20 years later Eng. on

business in America. Visits Indian. Greets him with
"How!" Indian – fried!" They howled!

4
THURSDAY

Recorder was good for once. New piece which is very
nice. Hilarious English lesson over meanings of words!
FIGURE. More revision. Everyone is getting very
edgy as MOCK starts on Tuesday. Liberation Day –
19th Feb. Newspapers printed threat to kill the Queen.
Seems it isn't a lot of twaddle after all. Some German
Fanatic. Great precautions being taken. Don't, myself,
think it'll come to anything.

5
FRIDAY

Everyone packed huge satchels tonight – doubt if
they'll be unpacked! Got M a token for the cinema for
her birthday and a cute card. Bought exam. skirt and
narrow green waspie. Washed the mop. Listened to the
radio – Ron and Eth a scream. Another plane crash on
mud flats. Papers say Q. Eliz. is having a tiring time of
it. Bet she's thoroughly fed up with this tour.

6
SATURDAY

Did all chores as Mum had to go to Grans. Tried to
revise in afternoon but not much good. Mum made
some of those delicious shortbreads – mmmmmm! Had
great fun watching Pal & Joan revising! Good Archer
programme. Have nearly got that plane off the mud
flats. G got a new lamp stand on Thurs – super.

7
SUNDAY

Liz & Margaret came up for forgotten French book in afternoon – what a mess in nylons and lipstick! Had a luxurious bath. Ellen didn't come.

8
MONDAY

Last lessons before exams – last minute advise – last frantic cramming! Wish they were over. Royal Scott [train] crashed yesterday. More pictures of a cool and charming Queen of England. Wish it was as hot here. Didn't do any Geog revision but Latin. It's a bit late now though. Well, I can just do my best. I loath & hate Latin. Especially the exam.

9
TUESDAY

Geog exam wasn't very good; nothing to get your teeth in – too scattered. The Ordinance Survey map was wicked. The Latin exam was putrid – awful. Couldn't do any of it. Dramatic Society great fun. Lots of snow today – several villages snowed up. Laurence Olivier was in "Marcine" tonight and was very good. I must read that book, by R.L.S.

10
WEDNESDAY

Spent free morning in half hearted revision for Algebra. The Algebra exam wasn't awful but it could have been better. Most people thought it was putrid however. Didn't hear the play as revising then went to bed early. A fortnight today the exams will be all over bar the shouting. The biology people say that the exam was awful. The weather is much warmer. Very hot in Sydney by newspapers.

11
THURSDAY

O my sainted aunt! That Geometry! I was in a panic by the time it was half over. I could do nothing. Some of the girls just drew. Everyone agrees it was awful, wicked. I never thought I'd fail a Maths exam, I usually get well over 80. The French was mediocre. Never can tell with French. O that Geometry – it was really fantastic!

12
FRIDAY

The Eng-lang paper wasn't bad at all – in fact quite good as exams go. For the essay I wrote "On wearing Uniform." But o boy the History – it was smashing. Wrote 11 pages. I could have done anything on that lovely paper. I did the map question too. Take it from hear was very good.

13
SATURDAY

Helped mum in morning as usual then slogged at Science all afternoon – with intervals of sneaking stuff from the larder and reading "We didn't mean to go to sea." Yes! You've guessed how much revision I did! Still, I did do some. Pud was at Joans so all was quiet on the western front.

14
SUNDAY

Shirley brought me a lovely brooch of shaped iron. Just

what I wanted. She saw it and knew it was just the sort of thing I love. Very decent.

15
MONDAY

Science wasn't as bad as I thought it would be although the chemistry was not very "nace". Spent afternoon in revision for English. Dashed home to hear the play which was very good indeed. It was about a lawyer who was prosecuting a bloke for a murder he hadn't done, then this lawyer is put in same circumstances – in end both get off.

16
TUESDAY

Art exam was not very good. I did "Rescue from Fire". Not very good. No boards, had to get own stuff – disgusting. English Literature was not bad but preferred language. Listened to Laurence Olivier and it was very good. Exams are slowly but surely creeping past! Just imagine, this time next week they'll all be over & will know some results (!)

17
WEDNESDAY

French exam this safternoon. Wasn't very easy – the second translation was much too hard. The Dictée wasn't bad but some quite difficult words in it. Revised for only 2 lessons in the morning – had dancing for one and had a good time and games for another. Sloshed around on top pitch with M and Janet. Revised Latin very little – spent evening reading "Womans", and listened to radio. Did not have play on since it is exams, but looking forward to it next week after they are finished.

18
THURSDAY

Auntie Florrie was found dead this morning, poor old thing. Ruptured Heart. She left no will either. Mum was very upset. They came for her first of all. I never thought Aunty Florrie would die for ages. Naturally had no time for revision tonight. Didn't get the tea over until 7 oclock. RIP.

19
FRIDAY

Aunty Jean came for funeral. Finished exams thank goodness me! Arithmetic was autrocious. Have done terrible in Maths – usually do so well. Went to the Dentist – awfully nice chap, young and Scotch. Had three minor fillings. Bought some magazines to relax tonight – but so busy making meals that I didn't.

20
SATURDAY

Had a hectic morning doing housework and trying to get dinner for 5. Managed somehow and there were no complaints. Mum & A.J at A.F's most of time. Dad and I bumped into them in afternoon and I joined them to help Mum buy a grey hat for funeral. She got a nice one. Have awful cold.

21
SUNDAY

Another day of washing dishes and getting meals. Mum & Aunty Jean went to see Aunty F's relatives.

Shirley came up. Gordon is very callous and flippant.

22
MONDAY

Everyone very relieved exams over. Only got one result Chemistry = 55% and was quite pleased because highest was pretty low. No one passed in Physics in 2nd Div! Bad lookout for us even if we are 1st div. Had a concert this afternoon from a quartet of 2 violins, viola & cello. It was very enjoable.

23
TUESDAY

Results rolling in! Algebra, 6th = 74%. Not bad. Latin = 55% Thrilled! Hardly any passed. Eng Literature, Top = 79% but Lang. 4th = 60% beat M. History top = 85% smashing! French 12th = 61%. Geography, disgusting, 2nd = 67% Have been alternately thrilled, depressed, excited disappointed today. Some haven't passed in anything.

24
WEDNESDAY

Awful to see some poor devils crying when they add fail after fail to their results, especially hard workers like Pat Baty. Got last of results – Physics got 71% – 3rd. So thats all the results. M and Marion and I all have nine passes and together with Grenfell have 68% top of form. Some poor devils have failed on the whole. There are going to be some scathing remarks at the end of term! The play was very poor so knocked it off. Usually very good. Had hair cut & washed. The new Berktex shop is super.

25
THURSDAY

What ructions in recorder!! M & I were howling at Miss Simpson & the rest & they were so funny! Any way, she lost her temper & roared at M that she'd better be quiet. Well! We just <u>couldn't</u> stop. Ever felt like that? So she got madder & told M she'd better be quiet or shed slap her face – Kindness! M had to flee, half hysterical, and I was left to face the music!

26
FRIDAY

Half term today and Monday. Helped mum in morning then went up town. Went to library & got a good book then got some petersham for skirt band. Then went to flics to see "All the brothers were valiant" at Lonsdale. Fair to good. Had a smashing "Bramble" Ice, it was super. Just bramble flavoured icecream but smashing.

27
SATURDAY

Read the book I got yesterday. It was very good but not enough tortures! What a carry on in Egypt with Neguib & Nasser! Talk about laugh! They're like a pair of comics but the situation is serious I suppose. The cartoonists are loving it and producing some real howlers.

28
SUNDAY

Shirley brought some magazines and I had a good time reading them. Ellen didn't come. Weather very cold and very snowy! Lovely!

MARCH
1954

1
MONDAY
St. David's Day

Had a real go at the housework this morning while
Mum did the washing. The new mop is super, so
is the U-banks sweeper - such a lot of labour
saved! Broke off to listen to "Mrs Dales Diary"
for a cup o' char. We're real old gossips! Fred is
<u>hopeless</u> she does nothing. Did all the ironing
which was a nice change.

2
TUESDAY

Dramatic Society was a riot! I missed my cue - I was
miles away - four times! And that love scene!
Miss Storer got married on Saturday - it seems to
have been a potty wedding - she's slightly off the
beam anyway. Talking of weddings, Virginia
Mackenna got married yesterday. It's lovely to
have the exams behind - oh got 5 T(top) & 6T ART.

3
WEDNESDAY
Ash Wednesday

Woke to a white world today. The snow is really thick
and some of the country girls had a job getting in.
The trees and fields at school are a perfect picture.
The branches are so delicate and covered with snow
they look lovely against the heavy grey sky. They
let us out quarter of an hour early to play
snowballs — what took them? I have started
to listen to "The Archers" a story of country folk.
It's quite good. Everywhere you go today you're met
with a cold snowball in the neck! It's fun really.

1
MONDAY

Had a real go at the housework this morning while Mum did the washing. The new mop is super, so is the U-bank sweeper – such a lot of labour saved! Broke off to listen to "Mrs Dales Diary" for a cup o'char. We're real old gossips! Pud is hopeless she does nothing. Did all the ironing which was a nice change.

2
TUESDAY

Dramatic Society was a riot! I missed my cue – I was miles away – four times! And that love scene! Miss Storer got married on Saturday – it seems to have been a potty wedding – shes slightly off the beam anyway. Talking off weddings, Virginia Mackenna got married yesterday. Its lovely to have the exams behind – oh got 87 (top) & 67 ART.

3
WEDNESDAY

Woke to a white world today. The snow is really thick and some of the country girls had a job getting in. The trees and fields at school are a perfect picture. The branches are so delicate and covered with snow they look lovely against the heavy grey sky. They let us out quarter of an hour early to play snowballs – what took them? Have started to listen to "The Archers" a story of country folk. Its quite good. Everywhere you go today you're met with a cold snowball in the neck! Its fun really.

4
THURSDAY

The snow is hard today. Most of the roads & pavements
are ankle deep in sloggy slimy slush. There is a slight
drizzle too. We had dancing instead of gym. It was
quite good. We did some jazzy American ones, but they
are not very good to dance to. Recorder was relatively
quiet today! Miss S is worried because the festival is
only 2 weeks off. The piece "Pipes are Sweet " isn't bad.

5
FRIDAY

Threw my books in the corner tonight – cant be
bothered to do any prep after the exams. Its soft having
them so early because no one feels like doing any work!
Had a nice cosy evening listening to the radio, reading
and drinking lime juice cordial and eating chocolate
cream biscuits. Mmmm! Pud & Dad went to the flics
to see Rob Roy.

6
SATURDAY

Went to town in afternoon and got a book at the library.
Had a browse round town, looking in the windows. I
think I'll save and buy a suit for Easter – cant get jeans
I want anywhere. Later read the book – The Village –
which was rather good – very ordinary but it rang true.

7
SUNDAY

Shirley was up & shes just had 2 teeth out and feels
awful! Ellen has had the flu so she wasn't here. Weather
blustery and cold.

8
MONDAY

Discussing in Scripture with Miss Cottrell wether Pools betting is a good or evil or harmless occupation. All thought it wasn't good but split on whether it was harmless or evil. Most of our fathers are fillers-in, but decided it wasn't harmless as so many workers are employed in various jobs on the Pools! Surely they would be better employed on the Countries work?

9
TUESDAY

It was the annual Grammar–High hockey match today & the boys beat us by 3:1. They won by shear weight and speed, I think. Had a good chat in Art as no one was sitting with us. The papers have pictures of the Sultan of somewhere all blood, after being shot by an assassin. They have a picture of his face too. Not very "nace" as Chester Coote would say.

10
WEDNESDAY

Real feeling of Spring in The Air today. Nicer day than many we get in our so called Summer. Went to see Miss C to be excused from School Council because of recorder. Said she was very sorry because the form could always depend on me to speak my mind, for which Im well known! Had a lovely chat for an hour in Physics while waiting for Faradays Law experiment to work. Blessedly, it did! We're all a bit fed up with school at present. The aftermath of exams I suppose. We all wish the holidays would hurry up and the Tennis Season start.

11
THURSDAY

Another gorgeous day! Just like summer. We had outdoor gym and Athletics. Had a super time. Miss Simpson rattled again at recorder. Im leaving after the festival! Another little girl in Australia tried to kiss the Queen, getting a bit stale! Gordon has finished painting the bookshelves and they look very nice. The best hard court was put up today – it makes it more like summer than ever!

12
FRIDAY

Good weather continued though March wind prevailed. Dramatic Soc. Because match last Tuesday. The play is beginning to go with a swing. I like my part very much but I shant enjoy wearing beard & whiskers! It makes ones face feel as though it is in a vice. No books on Tuesday. Two rehersals next week and one going over property cupboard. Super Art chatting lesson!

13
SATURDAY

Bought absolutely super blouse today – white broderie anglaise with sweet collar and cap sleeves with bobbles on. Its smashing – used up all my pocket money and had to borrow from Mum but worth every penny of it. Recorder practise this morning. She said she had a bonny lot – if brainless!

14
SUNDAY

Ellen came today, looking lovely in a reddy brown dress

with white collar. She is a little minx tho'! Another
'plane smash yesterday. Terrible.

15
MONDAY

What a day! Everything went wrong. Missed bus,
forgot gloves, forgot recorder, had sinus, and as a result
was in a flaming temper all day. Discussed churchgoing
in Scripture. Decided today empty churchs would be
filled if all different sects merged into one. People have
been trying to do this for generations, however. Miss
Cottrell looked utter mess. Disgusting!

16
TUESDAY

Had a smashing time at Dramactic Soc. Jenifer Sharp,
the hero, and me, the lover, had a super sword fight.
Brought a sword home for Gordon to copy for me. The
Queen has been warned against all sorts of things on
her tour of Western Australia because of polio. It would
be dreadful if she caught it. Lots more lovely pictures
of her and the Duke.

17
WEDNESDAY

The play is in its sticky stage – everyone is fed up with
it and noone is acting very well. We have 3 rehersals
then the dress rehersal – that's a fortnight today. We
are doing it on the Friday after. The weather is lovely
today. Wish three weeks today was here as we would
have broke up. I've never wanted to break up before but
I do this term – it seems such a drag when exams were

so early. The Paris people are beginning to get excited.
Jenifer will be going soon as well. Wish I was going –
but I will one day. <u>Definetly</u>!!!

18
THURSDAY

Miss Simpson in a nervous mood with the big day of
the festival tomorrow. We had a big row over what to
wear because Doreen wanted to wear a grey skirt and
we were all wearing gymslips. Theyre both school
uniform. Finally, had it symmetrically arranged – 3
wearing skirts on back row and rest gym slips. The
piano pupils are all on edge! So are we.

19
FRIDAY

Well, the festival went off okay. We got 85, second team
82. But we didn't deserve it. M was second in the solo
piano, out of 17, and Ann Greenop romped home with
the cup. Joan, Puds Pal, was 3rd out of 17 in her class.
Amy won, & Amy also won the duet in her class. M &
Hilary Jex were 4th in their duet out of 5. Surprised
that they didn't do better. J 2nd in duet.

20
SATURDAY

Read Jane Eyre today. Was amazed to find that I quite
enjoyed it. The last time I read it, when I was about
10, I loathed it – indeed, I never finished it. Gordons
birthday today. Pud & I bought him a 10/- book token
between us. Mum & Dad a pair of slippers. Shirley a
super pullover in fawn – really sporty. I'd like one myself.

21
SUNDAY

Had a small family party for Gordons birthday. Had peaches, jelly, egg & cress sandwiches, scrummy cream cakes etc. Finish D. Baders life (still alive!) story. Super.

22
MONDAY

Miss Cottrell had to show someone around school so had a super lesson just talking – wonderful waste of time! Jen was telling me all about her coming trip to South France. Shes been getting all sorts of new things for it. Suit – dresses – skirts etc. Shes beginning to get excited. The Paris people are also; tho they wont have such a good time as Jen. Parents meeting tonight. Wonder how they're getting on?

23
TUESDAY

Mum enjoyed the "At Home" last night. Wouldn't tell me what anyone had said, but managed to squeeze it out of her eventually. Everyone seems to have said lots of nice things. Mrs Henry said I wouldn't be satisfied with Art alone because my brain was too good. I'm inclined to agree with her, tho I don't know about the brain! Mrs Blake said I was VG at History. Everyone says I'm very imaginative

24
WEDNESDAY

and strongwilled. Miss C said I would make a name for myself one day. Wish I could believe that! My poor old sword broke today! Everyone howled. The play was

quite good tonight "The Heiress" with Celia Johnson.
Hardly did anything in Physics – just listened to her
blaahing away about batteries etc. Under fifteen team
beat St. Gabriels by 11–0! The 1st eleven beat Wigton
Friends by 7–1. Made an appointment for my hair. A
fortnight today we'll have broken up for the Easter hols!
Hurray! Love end of term!

25
THURSDAY

Gordon & Mum cleared sitting room today for start of
stripping & redecorating it. Lousy paper on at present.
Yellow with whopping roses in the corners! Back to
normal in recorder. Pud got a super school story from
school library today & couldn't stop reading it – haven't
read a school story for simply years. Used to read
nothing but once upon a time.

26
FRIDAY

Soppy Art lesson – drawing daffodils! What a milksop
job. But 1 compensation – only enough daffodils for us
too share, so needed to talk to each other! Progressing
with sitting room. Finished the school story. A fortnight
today they'll be leaving for Paris! – I think I think about
it more than they do! Wish I was going. Will some day,
I swear.

27
SATURDAY

Stripped a wall & a half this morning! Is my back
sore! Got telegram from A. Jean saying they're coming
tonight – Ye Gods! They came at 8 pm exactly. I nearly

had claustrophobia, all being in one room. The room is gradually getting stripped. Joan had her slacks on today so Pud is all for a pair!

28
SUNDAY

Had a super drive with Uncle Dave this afternoon. Went to Caldbeck. Gorjeous view of countryside. The weather was pretty reasonable too. Very nice.

Margaret aged fifteen, posing for her brother Gordon, a trainee photographer, in the countryside

29
MONDAY

Empire Windrush on fire today. Newspapers full of complementary things about the behaviour of the passengers – they were apparently wonderful. Lessons dragging – wish it was the end of term. Busied myself getting costume spruced up for dress rehearsal tomorrow. Paul Temple started again tonight – very good as usual. New Paul Temple – Peter Coke, VG.

30
TUESDAY

What a dress rehearsal! It was putrid. No one knew their words, no one was picking up their cues fast enough – it was terrible. Lost rain coat belt in general shemousal but found it later. Hope the play goes better on Friday – everyone will have too make a real effort. Practising hard for Choir competition – not bad our choir. Pretty big.

31
WEDNESDAY

Got out of afternoon lessons for play practice. Going much better thank goodness. My fight with Jen is going very well & we've thought up quite a few funny bits to put in. Struggled on with beastly Geometry for prep – loath the stuff. The play was awfully good – by Nicholas Monsarrat the famous author. Got out of Physics for afternoon for rehersal of play – its coming along a lot better but still lacks that extra something that makes a play a success. Perhaps we'll get it on the day.

APRIL
1954

1
THURSDAY

The L VI concert was terrific! Superb skits on the whole of school life - especially school dinners Irene Graham was wonderful - wrote, produced & acted in it. Really awfully clever. They made £12 for Dr. Barnados which was awfully good. Skit on recorders, so Miss Simpson said we couldn't have them after that! Thanks to the L VI!

2
FRIDAY

Well! our play was the most glorious success! They laughed from start to finish. They roared at my love scene and clapped my exit uproariously! Gosh, its lovely to be clapped off stage. Then our fight was wonderful - they roared & clapped & Jen & I loved every minute of it. All day people came up laughing & congratulating me. Success is sweet!

3
SATURDAY

The choirs last practice was this morning. It went off pretty well, I think. Pud got a new coat today - camel cloth, belted, large pockets. Quite nice. She's awfully excited about going to London. Jen left last night for the South of France. Horrible day - rain & cold wind all day.

4
SUNDAY
Passion Sunday

Better sort of day - sunny but windy with squalls all day. Prudence Parkinson died today It's terrible. She was our Head Girl 2 years ago.

1
THURSDAY

The LVI concert was terrific! Superb skits on the whole
of school life – especially school dinners. Irene Graham
was wonderful – wrote, produced & acted in it. Really
awfully clever. They made £12 for Dr. Barnardo's which
was awfully good. Skit on recorders, so Miss Simpson
said we couldn't have them after that! Thanks to the LVI!

2
FRIDAY

Well! Our play was the most glorious success! They
laughed from start to finish. They roared at my love
scene and clapped my exit uproariusly! Gosh, its lovely
to be clapped off stage. Then our fight was wonderful –
they roared & clapped & Jen & I loved every minute of
it. All day people came up laughing & congratulating
me. Success is sweet!

3
SATURDAY

The choirs last practice was this morning. It went off
pretty well, I think. Pud got a new coat today – camel
cloth, belted, large pockets. Quite nice. She's awfully
excited about going to London. Jen left last night for the
South of France. Horrible day – rain & cold wind all day.

4
SUNDAY

Better sort of day – sunny but windy with squalls all day.
Pruedence Pattinson died today. Its terrible. She was
our Head Girl 2 years ago.

5
MONDAY

Well, the choir competition went off okay. Lanercost won, we were second, Linstock third and Netherby [school houses] last. A. Nan & Mike arrived today – A. Nan as elegant, slim and perky as usual. Mike a bit taller but not half as big as me. Listened to all the gossip with A. Nan and A. Laura and Mum. Paul Temple was as good as usual. Good serial.

Margaret, left, cousin Michael, sister Pauline

6
TUESDAY

Broke up today. VIth gave concert this morning. Not bad but not as good as Lower VI tho. Good breaking up ceremony as usual. Lots of cheers etc – even for that old devil Cottrell! Aunty Laura was up to see Aunty Nan so they had a good chat. Mike had spent the day doing housework! Report okay – 5 A's, 5 B's. Puds quite good. L. Olivier good.

7
WEDNESDAY

Mike, Pud & I were treated to the flics this afternoon by A. Nan. It was jolly good – Houdini. Tony Curtis & Janet Leigh were both awfully good. Arrowhead with it wasn't bad – good colour and plenty to watch. Shirley came up to be introduced to Aunty Nan so had a pleasant evening – if a bit rowdy at times. A. Nan had been to see an old friend who had piled her with eggs, ham and cakes, so had a jolly good scoff! Missed the play of course. Slept with A. Nan because Pud kicked her all last night. She's an awful sleeper.

8
THURSDAY

Spent the afternoon taking photos. First, Aunty Nan in the lounge – a real studio portrait. What a carry on! We all teased her so that she could hardly keep her face straight. Then went to the bay & had all photos taken. Gordons a super photographer. Mike & A.N & I went to A. Laura's then to the mitre where Mick and I wallowed in lemonade.

9
FRIDAY

Saw Pud & the Marshallsays off safely. Pud's awfully excited about her London visit. Wish I was going to

London. Girls set off for Paris today. One day I'll visit all these places, and more. Bought a magazine and settled down with an orange for the afternoon. The house is strangely quiet without Mike & Pud. (Nice and restful too, thank goodness!).

10
SATURDAY

Went to town with Mum for a blazer, but they had not any in, unfortunately. Got two good books from the library – a Pollyanna book with Puds junior ticket & a John Creasey one. The weather is very good today apart from traditional April showers and a stiff breeze. Washed my mop – cant do a thing.

11
SUNDAY

Read the Creasey book – pretty good. It must take him ages to write them, you know. Went to church as usual. Special Palm Sunday Service.

12
MONDAY

Helped Mum all morning – she did the washing and me the housework. Gran went into hospital today at 4 o'clock. It will be a change for her, poor old thing. Had Ellen this afternoon after cleaning my bike. She's a real Madam. We had our tea – toast made with the inexpert assistance of the Pickle [dog]. What a job I had getting her home! She collected quite a lot to go with her!

13
TUESDAY

Usual housework with break for Mrs Dales Diary.

Went to the cinema in afternoon – Million £ note with Gregory Peck. I think he's wonderful, terrific. The film was very amusing. Wanted to take Mum but she was going to see Gran who is getting on all right, so bought her some delicious oozy cream cakes instead. Went to see Grandpa in evening. Had hot bath & early night.

14
WEDNESDAY

Have been so used to having a 34-24-34 figure that when I was trying on my summer things I really had a fit when I couldn't get them on. Measured myself and horrors – 36-28-38!! Awful. So on diet. Half grapefruit for breakfast. 1 boiled egg + ½ slice of bread for dinner & 3 slices of brown bread + 1 cup of milk & sugarless tea + 1 plain bun. Determined to keep it up for 14 days. Weight = 9 st 7! Must get it down to 8 st. Went to Jeans for afternoon – took John his Easter Egg. The play – The Net – was very good indeed. Still can't decide whether he lived or died in the end though.

15
THURSDAY

Lovely day today, in spite of strong wind. Took a nightie to City General in morning for Gran. Went a very long detour to Jeans in afternoon – round by Newby, Moorhouse & Cumersdale Way; it was gorgeous – lovely blue sky, green fields etc.

16
FRIDAY

Lovely day – at least, lovely morning, as it dulled in this afternoon, although it was still warm. Went to Church in morning. Dad was in his blessed garden all day – as were most men. Gordon was doing Granda's garden. Letter from Pud. She seems to have had a whale of a time in London – she saw 3 personages – Prince Charles, Prin. Anne & Anthony Eden.

17
SATURDAY

The Wallaces arrived at 8.15. Davids girl friend is very petite – 5 foot – slim, & pretty. Seems very nice altogether. Went to see Grandma this afternoon. I never want to go their again. All the patients made me feel sick. One woman has been in 35 years! Her face is awful. Poor Devils. How I admire nurses but I <u>couldn't be</u> one.

18
SUNDAY

Went a lovely run to Silloth & along coast with Grace, David, Dad & Uncle Dave. Rather Blustery there, but gorgeous all the way back. Nicest weather at Easter for years.

19
MONDAY

Uncle Dave & I drove Mum & Aunty Jean to Silloth in the afternoon. It was a gorgeous day – much better than yesterday even. We found a nice spot on the top of a mossy bank overlooking the sand & the sea. It was wonderful lying their, with the sun beating down from a cloudless sky & the sea sparkling like a silver band before us; the salty & piny smells were super.

20
TUESDAY

Today Un.D & A.J, Mum & I went off to the Lakes. It was another perfect day &we took a picnic tea. The drive was superb. We picniced in Lodore grounds then I climbed to the top of Cauder Crag. The view was enchanting – the blue, blue lakes rippling in the sun, backed by the mountains – all green and yellow and red like a patch work quilt & behind me the red woods with the trees outlined against the sky. Everything was spread out like a living map.

21
WEDNESDAY

I yearned for the mountains today. I must go back soon. The Wallaces left today & I went a bike ride, it was such a lovely day. I meandered through country lanes with the fields on either side until I came to Burgh marsh road. I walked to the coast line and lay on the hut, gloriying in the warmth & beauty – all was so peaceful, so beautiful. I cycled back slowly, stopping every now & again to look back on the sea, & the silver pool where I rested and had an orange. I relaxed in bed, bruised & scratched from climbing on Tuesday & felt how good life was. The play was a fitting climax to a perfect day. "Stop Press Murder."

22
THURSDAY

Today wasn't so warm, but still very nice. Housework in morning, as usual. Spent afternoon reading a "Woman" & eating smarties & doughnuts in the garden on a deck chair. Granda came up in the evening to tell us how Grandma was. We were all in a giddy mood this evening. The papers are full of the Petrov affair; looks fishy.

23
FRIDAY

Another Russian "surrendered" to Americans in West Germany. Wonder whats cooking? Pud came back this afternoon – old cheery self. Had a row with Gordon this afternoon, old beast. She brought some lovely apples with her. Sick of that old beast Gordon Big Mr Know All. And so Smug! Poor old Shirley.

24
SATURDAY

Went to town with Mum to see if we could get her a coat but couldn't see one she or I fancied. She hasn't had a coat for years. Tried on my Summer things – wont look at me! All too tight. So sold one dress to Pud for 15/- it was 32/6 & I've only worn it 7 times. Both my skirts too small – Ye gods, wish I'd stopped growing.

25
SUNDAY

Australian–Russian split – wonder if war is imminent? Very cold again today, but sun got out.

26
MONDAY

A lovely day, but cold. Did housework while Mum washed – Pud being an unhelpful minx. However, she partially atoned for it by treating Mum & I to the flics this afternoon – The Kidnappers. It was an excellent film. The acting of Vincent Winter was very touching.

Really, there was not much story but we thoroughly enjoyed it.

27
TUESDAY

Returned to school in high spirits. Everyone full of holiday yarns – particularly the Paris Girls. They seem to have had a wonderful time, lucky dogs. Swimming starts tomorrow, but I seem to be the only one from our lot going 2nd period, although Mary & Jenifer & Hazel might. Had a super Art lesson – supposedly drawing twigs but really, talking! It was a lovely sunny evening.

28
WEDNESDAY

Grandma died today.

Had a super swimming lesson with Mary & the rest. Miss Taylor (she's wonderful!) gave Mary & I special things to do because we were the only ones who could swim well – handstands, somersaults, lifesaving, underwater swimming, diving for pennies. We thoroughly enjoyed ourselves. But it was Maths afterwards & old Haigh nattered away because we were a few minutes late.

29
THURSDAY

Had a super gym lesson today. First ran round the playing fields, then practised long jump then came inside and did longfly & handspring & crows nest. Tired out after we finished. The weather is lovely & sunny, tho' still rather cold. The tennis courts look lovely and inviting – itching for a game. Lousy old recorder as usual – annoyed her as much as possible.

30
FRIDAY

Mum got a lovely new coat (about time too) of a lovely oatmeal shade and she has a lovely amethyst hat to go with it. Had a super game of tennis. Ann Greenop & I played against Skinny & Janet. Beat them easily 6–1. Skinny smashed a window tho. The ball just whammed past Ann & I and went right through a pane! What a shock the people inside got!

MAY
1954

1 MAY
SATURDAY

Did Act prep. & French in afternoon, but soon finished so went shopping with Mum locally. West Bromwich Albion beat Preston N.E. 3-2 in Wembley Cup Final, but not very exciting except for the actual goals. Rain most of day. Branda's lost without Branding. They all went to the cemetery in the evening.

2
SUNDAY
2nd after Easter

Went a long, long tramp this afternoon. It rained but I thoroughly enjoyed myself. Brought back a lovely armful of leaks & branches for the sittingroom.

3
MONDAY
Bank Holiday, Scotland

Rainy again today, tho' bright spells occasionally. We are revising in quite a few subjects now, & getting through a lot of work. S.C. starts on May 31st & goes on to 2nd July. What a grind! Will have a lovely lazy time afterwards tho [I hope!]. Exam that takes me is French oral. Gossiped at corner for the 410 min in rain!

4
TUESDAY

Another rainy day, but many more bright periods. Work is speeding up no end now. Last minute panic! Saw lovely pictures of the Royal Family at Malta on todays front page. They're nearly home now. I think I'll emigrate to Australia or America & work on the internal Airlines. Nice warm weather & Travel, both of which I crave. I must Travel (only warm places)

1
SATURDAY

Did Art prep. & French in afternoon, but soon finished so went shopping with Mum locally. West Bromwich Albion beat Preston N.E. 3–2 in Wembley Cup Final, but not very exciting except for the actual goals. Rain most of day. Granda's lost without Grandma. They all went to the cemetery in the evening.

2
SUNDAY

Went a long, long tramp this afternoon. It rained but I thoroughly enjoyed myself. Brought back a lovely armful of leafs & branches for the sittingroom.

3
MONDAY

Rainy again today, tho bright spells occasionally. We are revising in quite a few subjects now, & getting through a lot of work. S.C. starts on May 31st & goes on to 2nd July. What a grind! Will have a lovely lazy time afterwards tho (I hope!). Exam that scares me is French oral. Gossiped at corner for 1 hr & 10 mins in rain!

4
TUESDAY

Another rainy day, but many more bright periods. Work is speeding up no end now. Last minute panic! Some lovely pictures of the Royal Family at Malta on todays front page. Theyre nearly home now. I think I'll emigrate to Australia or America and work on the internal Airlines. Nice warm weather & Travel, for which I crave. I <u>must</u> travel (only warm places)!

5
WEDNESDAY

Tore down to baths & was in first. Only decent time was before rest arrived. Real scandal – Dulcie in first six! Disgraceful – Joyce Davidson could beat her with one hand behind her back. Everyone in an uproar over it. Physics lousy – don't seem to be getting anywhere and all this tommy rot passes over my head about Light. Another awful rainy cold day. Ruined Tennis after school. Couldn't get down to revision – just one of those nights. Must start revising soon – only 4 weeks left!

The play was very Good. These new plays are.

6
THURSDAY

Got chucked out of recorder tonight for imitating Polly Wynne and was jolly glad. Wish I could get her roused more often to chuck me out. Played Tennis instead of Gym but it was a howling gale & almost impossible. Double English on Kipps. Just think – 2 months today the SC will be over! Hurrah! Made a start on revision but didn't get very far! The weather is atrocious.

7
FRIDAY

Wonderful feat accomplished yesterday by Roger Bannister who ran the mile in 3 mins 59.4 secs! At last, the 4 minute mile. Front Page headlines & pictures. Glad an Englishman got it before anyone else. Stayed and played Tennis after school with Joyce Shakespeare. Beat her, but we hardly did anything for laughing! Shes a born comic. <u>Must</u> have a raquet – wish I had.

8
SATURDAY

Wasted a lovely day. I don't know – everything seemed wrong. My hair was a mess. I hadn't my blazer or a summer frock, and I just wept all afternoon. It seems silly know but I was just fed up to the teeth with life. Went a walk in the evening, in old raincoat, and the countryside was so beautiful it compensated.

9
SUNDAY

Papers full of the Russian Spy Scandal in London. They've been ordered out of the country. Given 3 weeks. What with all the other carry ons …!

10
MONDAY

Perfectly glorious day – sunny & hot. Put everyone in a good temper! 3 weeks to the School Cert and the teachers are fairly putting the pressure on! Went for my blazer but it wasn't big enough. Heigh Ho! I <u>wish</u> I had it. Played Tennis after prep for ½ hour against cemetery wall. Started School Cert revision tonight. Did some Physics.

11
TUESDAY

Stayed after school and had a good game with M. It was another lovely day. Whats happened – 2 lovely days in succession! Played Tennis against wall for ½ hr or so. The papers have pictures of the Royal Family at Gibraltar and they are nearly home. It will be lovely to have them back again – it doesn't seem 6 mths since they were away. Tempus fugit!

12
WEDNESDAY

Did not go to baths because of Parliament, but swotted up last weeks physics prep. It was another lovely day today – really hot. That old beast Cottrell says we cant roll our sleeves up, nor can we wear gym blouses. That lousy so and so stinks. She really <u>is</u> the limit – and she looks such a slut too. Physics quite good this afternoon. How we stand and gossip at the corner. Its an institution, so all the mistresses say! We find plenty to talk about. The play wasn't very good tonight. Soon the rep company will be back. Mean to see every performance.

13
THURSDAY

Recorder "blumin orful". The weather has broke too, but it is still warm. Had a usual fortnight letter from Gill – usual pleasant gossip. She's got another boy friend – these soppy girls! She might be able to visit me this year if Gordon goes to Norway. It would be great fun – I could take her all over the place, The Lakes, Silloth, Burgh, etc. So heres hoping!

14
FRIDAY

Did last of plant drawing in Art today – a rhododendrum which was quite nice to draw. Bought a "Woman" and read that in the evening, then drew wallflower for Art prep. Also took up hem of skirt for Pud. The weather is lousy. The first pictures of the Queens return are coming in – shes lovelier than ever & the kids are full of life. It will be nice to have her back.

15
SATURDAY

Mum & I went to town and bought me a lovely pale greeny blue cottony silk dress, with cap sleeves and full skirt. Also a pair of vivid turquoise jeans. Very daring! We finished up with tea in Binns – had a delicious meringue glace – 2 whopping helpings of meringue, a large blob of icecream & also orange squash!

16
SUNDAY

Isabel Goldsmith, the runaway bride, died yesterday after a Caesarean operation to deliver her baby. Really tragic. Almost fictious – the poor husband.

17
MONDAY

Quite a nice day. Pen nib broke in Chem. So they'll rush me 1/6 at Thurnams for that. Just like it to break before the SC. It'll take me ages to get this one broken in – its always scratchy to begin with. Did some Chemistry revision. More pictures of the Queen in this mornings papers. Anne is so like her, and Charles like his father. G bought a trick pen today!

18
TUESDAY

Took Gordons trick pen to school and had great fun with it. It exploded in Art and Mrs Henry was very interested in it! Had a lovely afternoon while others were at Hallé OC. Did prep 1st period, played Tennis on Creighton for 2nd and ½ of 3rd and sunbathed for rest of afternoon (supposed to be working!) Lovely –

worth being alive on such a glorius ~~night~~ day. Weather
lovely. Hallé was lousy.

19
WEDNESDAY

The play was very good tonight – "Crispins Day" with
Peter Coke. I hear that the Salisbury Arts one is too.
Good. Flew to baths, costume already on, and did
twenty six lengths before the others arrived and got
in. I'd like to go for a whole morning and do a mile
(76 lengths). Weather is lovely & sunny, although
dull at times. Sat on edge of Creighton Court and
watched Sheila & Co playing Tennis. They're a joy to
watch. Stayed and watched the 2nd six play Wigton
(Brookfield) 1st six. They got beaten but put up a jolly
good fight. If the 1st six had played they would have
knocked them into oblivion.

20
THURSDAY

At last! Hurray! Expelled – chucked out – of recorder
today! Final Blow Up! Read all about it! We had a
terrific row (Miss Simpson & I) and finally she said
I could go – forever! So I stood up & cheered and had
the class in stitches. She was furious. I wouldn't go back
if she crawled to me on her nyloned knees & begged
me. Will send a bunch of dandelions with "Goodbye
forever" on!!

21
FRIDAY

Played Tennis on Creighton with M until half past five.
Had a wonderful game. We were both playing pretty

well. My feet were killing me something chronic, so was glad to get to the Theatre & relax with Mary & Jennifer. The play – "The Love of Four Colonels" – was okay, but have seen better. The morales were a bit questionable! Half the school were there. Next week should be good.

22
SATURDAY

Puds birthday – sent her a Greetings Telegram. Came to arrangement with her – I give <u>her</u> 5/- for her birthday and she gives <u>me</u> 5/- for mine, because we're both hard up! Her and Joan went to the Theatre after a slap up tea. Did Art prep – Red Indians – the subject wasn't bad. Washed mop and listened to Saturday night theatre. Rest out.

23
SUNDAY

Horoscope for year in Dispatch: energetic year with considerable personal success. Hope it means the S.C! Express "prosperity". Pud & Joan enjoyed Theatre last night.

24
MONDAY

A blasted cuckoo woke me up this morning at 7'o-clock! Drat the bird. The orals started today – don't seem to have been so very bad. Am having mine tomorrow – Ugh! No one thinks of me being nervous – they say I haven't any nerves – but inside I <u>feel</u> <u>awful</u>. Wish it were over. Started on "Kipps" tonight. 5 weeks today......!

25
TUESDAY

Waking thought was not "its my birthday" but "it's the French oral!" Every card I opened heaped burning coals – "happy birthday" and "May this be the happiest of days" Ugh! Suffered something terrible before it (never nervous before!) but it wasn't really bad! It rained and blew all morning but after the oral the sun shone! It was a lovely evening too. Got on with Kipps. Not a bit like a birthday today! Got 14 cards, 5/- from M, ½ lb chocs from Pat & money.

26
WEDNESDAY

Took some photos of me to school and everyone went mad over them. Came back with none! Valerie Hepple in particular was struck with them & said "you know, you're awfully lucky – you've got some lovely clothes." I was astounded! So I told her it was only a Marks skirt and then she said: "But it's the way you wear them." What a nice compliment. But I've always thought I didn't suit anything! The play was very good – "Boys in Brown". Had a good swim at the baths – got there 3 mins after the bell! Miss Taylor just goggled & I said I was jet propelled! The weather has picked up and is lovely. Finished Kipps, thank goodness. Macbeth next.

27
THURSDAY

The blasted cuckoo woke me at <u>4.30am</u> this morning!

It haunts me – cant get to sleep anyhow. Drat the bird. Read Macbeth tonight. Didn't go to recorder, of course, but we were still talking when the recorder lot were getting out! Real old gossips! Hunted some more photos out to show Valerie – she wants them. Some quite funny ones among them.

28
FRIDAY

The Theatre was quite good, but the play itself was poor I thought. It was "The Man who came to Dinner." Michael Ingrams played the lead and was very good. The weather is dreadful. Spent Art lesson putting the things in the Gym for the school cert. It looks awful – row upon row of desks all with jars of water and drawing boards etc ready for the Art exam on Monday.

29
SATURDAY

Went to town to choose grate – got a lovely one. Dying to see it in. Bought a pair of buttercup yellow pyjamas and a natural coloured cardigan and a waist slip. The pyjamas are super. Swotting spasamodically in the afternoon & went hunting the cuckoo – with no luck – in evening. Weather picking up considerably.

30
SUNDAY

Gorgeous day. Lazed all afternoon in deck chair then went for a walk. Not long before the long fray begins!

BEGINNING OF SCHOOL CERTIFICATE

31
MONDAY

Well, the S.C. began today! It was Art all day, with Composition in the morning and poster in the afternoon. Both were quite good. For the Composition I did "In sunless glades amidst the shades the ancients tend their sacrificial fires." For the poster I did a holiday poster.

I quite enjoyed the papers, really lovely weather!

JUNE
1954

1 JUNE
TUESDAY

Art plant drawing in morning — Iris oo. Ugh! Had finished in an hour and quarter so had to sit doing nothing for an hour and ¼. Painted my hand! Off in the afternoon, so swotted Physics & Chemistry then read a Dennis Wheatly book. Wish I hadn't & had done more Science. It will be the worst exam, I'm sure. Don't know a bally thing about Chemistry.

2
WEDNESDAY

The Science was <u>awful</u>. I took one look at the blessed paper and just about passed out. Ye Gods! On tackling it I found that the Physics wasn't so bad except for the calculations but the Chemistry! Could only answer half of each of three! Everyone else was cursing too — some got on even worse than me. Gorgeous day. Just lay all afternoon in deck chair sun bathing — tan coming on grand. Went a walk in the cemetery with Brenda, and later to meet Mum. The weather really is marvellous. Had letter from Bill — usual friendly gossip, but short!

3
THURSDAY

The English Language stunk — it was putrid except for the essay. Wrote on "The schoolgirl of fiction and fact". Not bad. Another lovely day, so as it was Gordons half-day we went away up the river to the second waterfall and sunbathed all afternoon & paddled. But my conscience fairly smote me! Engl. Lit tomorrow. However, put in about 3 hrs in the evening

1
TUESDAY

Art plant drawing in morning – irises. Ugh! Had
finished in an hour and quarter so had to sit doing
nothing for an hour and ¼. Painted my hand! Off in
the afternoon, so swotted Physics and Chemistry then
read a Dennis Wheatly book. Wish I hadn't & had
done more Science. It will be the worst exam, I'm sure.
Don't know a bally thing about Chemistry.

2
WEDNESDAY

The Science was <u>awful</u>. I took one look at the blessed
paper and just about passed out. Ye Gods! On tackling
it I found that the Physics wasn't so bad except for the
calculations but the Chemistry! Could only answer half
of each of three! Everyone else was cursing too – some
got on even worse than me. Gorgeous day. Just lay all
afternoon in deck chair sun bathing – tan coming on
grand. Went a walk in the cemetery with Granda, and
later to meet Mum. The weather really is marvellous.
Had letter from Gill – usual friendly gossip, but short!

3
THURSDAY

The English Language stunk – it was putrid except for
the essay. Wrote on "The schoolgirl of fiction and fact."
Not bad. Another lovely day, so as it was Gordon's half-
day we went away up the river to the second waterfall and
sunbathed all afternoon & paddled. But my conscience
fairly smoted me! Engl. Lit tomorrow. However, put in
about 3 hrs in the evening.

4
FRIDAY

The Eng Lit paper was not bad, tho very vague which made it tricky. Best so far, bar Art. In afternoon (still lovely weather) Mary, Jen & I went swimming at the baths for an hour. Miss Taylor & the instructor were there. Bath to ourselves. Worked really hard, then Hazel joined us & we salamandered through town licking ices. Lorna tacked on & we spent an hour also in the Milk bar with pepsis & ice. Went to see Dr. in House in evening. VG.

5
SATURDAY

The weather is still very nice. Sunbathed all afternoon. Suntan coming on fine. Pud & Joan played all afternoon. Uneventful day. See in newspapers that Boko, the surviving Siamese twin, is doing well & there is a lovely photo of her. Listened to some of Saturday Night Theatre and washed my mop – it gets worse. Wrote to Gill inviting her for hols.

6
SUNDAY

Weather terrible. Read Sunday papers – usual stuff. Wish weather would go sunny again. Spent boring evening. Nice walk to Church.

7
MONDAY

Terrible weather for a Whit Monday. Mum & I went to see "Hobsons Choice" at the Lonsdale. It was very good indeed – John Mills was excellent. Pud is staying for today & the next two days at Joans, so I'll have some room in the bed for a change. Did some History in the evening – the exams seem miles away now. Silly having 4 ordinary days in middle.

8
TUESDAY

Went to town with mum this afternoon and after an exhausting trail round town got a very nice green mac at Richards. I'm an awful person to go shopping with, says Mum, because I'm so faddy & get so gloomy if I cant get what I'm looking for. Also got blazer at last, from Jespers. They are quick – managed to get me it by half term!!! Did some more History in the evening & read magazines.

9
WEDNESDAY

Drew £8.13.7d out of bank – amount over £100. £3 for mac and I spent the other £5.10s on a new raquet. Its super – a Dunlop Maxply, with red gut and light weight and thinnish grip. Just what I wanted. Also bought another pair of pyjamas – deep blue, with tie belt & white piping round edge. Its lovely to have a bit of money to spend! Came home & made myself bacon & egg and listened to Childrens Hour. Pud came home after a pleasant weekend (for me too!). Listened to play – Its an Ill wind – which was quite good but the reception was poor due to storms. Finished History before listening to the play. Weather bad.

10
THURSDAY

Nice to get back to school again. Always is. Weather

picked up in the afternoon, then broke in the evening. Got okay from Corporation to go ahead with Grate. Looking forward immensely to getting it in – I hate the old black monstrosity. All this due to money from Grandma left. As I write this the rain is lashing the lupins against the window and the trees are sagging with the wind. Lovely sort of atmosphere.

11
FRIDAY

Went to Theatre as usual tonight – & how it poured. We were all there by 6.30 so we had a stand until 7. We fairly got wet but the time passed quickly. Then, once inside, there was the mad dive for the front row. We all secured seats and talked & talked until that magical moment when the lights went down and the curtain rose. The play – The Living Room – was very good. Made you think.

12
SATURDAY

Did a little Geography in afternoon, but mostly read "Womans Own's". Listened to some of play, it was very good. Have to knock it off when Dad comes in, but its fun, although tantalising to make up the end. The weather was mediocre today. Gordon had a wedding at Scotby. Good day for it, esp. light for photos.

13
SUNDAY

Had a wander through the cemetery in the evening – its so lovely in parts with the trees overhead and the daisy sprinkled grass beneath. Its really a lovely place.

14
MONDAY

Got our new grate in today – its super! It really changes the whole room, it so nice. The weather was quite nice today, rather windy though. Played tennis early this morning because had to get up early and washed before they turned the water of to put the grate in. My Maxply is terrific. I love Tennis. Some Dutch Simese twins have been successfully separated – they look lovely.

15
TUESDAY

School cert. starts again tomorrow with French. Will be glad when its all over. I cross out each exam viciously as it passes on my timetable in red pencil. It poured down today. Did some Geog. in the evening. Was off in the afternoon & got literally soaked to the skin coming home. My blouse was wringing wet. Spent afternoon going over French grammar & vocabulary. Dismal!

16
WEDNESDAY

Well, we had French today. The Aural test was pretty lousy – it was far to long – but found afterwards that I had most of the questions right. The English into French was putrid, I thought. The essay questions were not bad, but I never can write French essays. In the afternoon, the dictée was not bad – in fact easier than a lot we have had for practise. I also thought that the french into english translations were okay, especially the second one which I thought quite easy. The comprehension, too, was a lot easier than might have been expected. On the whole, it was not bad.

17
THURSDAY

Geometry this morning! Ye gods! Couldn't do any of it in Section A, but Section B was a bit better. I've failed, of course, but I've done better than last time. The Arithmetic in the afternoon was super. It was all pretty straightforward, & Section A was easy. I reckon I've done quite well in that – I need to have done to pull that wicked Geometry up! Hope Algebra is like Arithmetic.

18
FRIDAY

What a disappointment the History was! I could do it, but there was nothing good – nothing, practically, on Italy, nothing on Bismarck and nothing on the Whigs. The only decent question was on Peel. Very disappointing, everybody agreed. Umpired double match – Joan & Dulcie beat Hazel & M 6–1. Played tennis in afternoon. Went to the theatre in evening "Private Lives" it was super. I had a smashing time.

19
SATURDAY

Did some Geog in afternoon, and a bit in the evening. Washed the "mop" in the evening – it gets worse every wash! Just like an old mop. Listened to a bit of the play, but the reception was so bad – storms I expect – that we could not make out anything so had to knock it off. The weather was pretty lousy today – wish it would pick up.

20
SUNDAY

Shirley up, of course, and admired the grate very much. Ellen was over too. She's a real little minx & tore some of my revision lists up – luckily only ones I had finished with!

21
MONDAY

The Algebra exam was very good, especially Section B – two of the 3 were ridiculously easy and reckon I must have pulled my Geometry up. Off in afternoon, so did World Geography. Listened to the play repeat in the afternoon – Someone at The Door – and it was super! Did not do much Geog in evening because Pud & Joan occupied the front room with their "swotting" (!).

22
TUESDAY

Off all day. Went in for a Geog lesson in morning (just looked over old papers to get used to them) and did housework in morning for Mum who was cleaning the larder. Gordon brought an old typewriter home yesterday, so spent half of afternoon practising on it – picked it up quite quickly and could do it with both hands by the evening. Did some more Geog. Wish it was over. Hope we get Lowlands of Scotland.

23
WEDNESDAY

The Geog was awful! The world map was feeble – no rivers to speak of and no well known latitudes and silly questions about animals "valuable to man" in certain places. The Ordinance survey was not bad but the Australian question was wicked. Just a mingy little bit of the north east coast given! The British Isles questions were not too good either. Aw hell! I thought Geog at least would be good. Went to town with Mum to have a dekko at carpets – some nice one's in Dan Johnsons. Listened to the play – The Middle Watch – which wasn't bad. Weather is terrible – cold and blustery.

24
THURSDAY

House work in morning. Went to library in afternoon and was lucky enough to get a Berkerley Gray book – "Operation Conquest" – and spent the rest of the afternoon reading it. It was super – dead thrilling. Went to theatre with Jen as she can't go tomorrow and didn't want to go by herself. It was super – Waters of the Moon – and I thoroughly enjoyed it. Michael Ingrams was especially good, I thought.

25
FRIDAY

Helped mum in morning (we fairly get along when there is two of us!) Went with Gordon to choose a picture for the wall above the fireplace. Got a lovely one in a white frame – called "The Road to the Sea" by R. Wintz. Could have bought the whole shop up, they have such beautiful pictures in Greys. Went to see "Young Bess" at the Palace in the evening with Pud – it was terrific – Jean Simmons was excellent.

26
SATURDAY

Collected dress pattern from Binns but could not find any cotton that I liked. Will just have to keep looking. Spent afternoon swotting Latin. Loath the beastly subject. Wish the exams were finished – fed up to the teeth with them. Not one decent one so far & I hardly think Latin will be the exception!!

27
SUNDAY

Shirley's sister Jennifer came to tea today. Tried to swot some Latin but did not succeed very much. Wish the beastly thing was over. The new curate has a very nice voice.

28
MONDAY

Latin was simply unspeakable! Never been more certain that I've failed an exam. Ye Gods! Wish I'd worked at the lessons instead of larking about. One comfort – everyone agreed. M's mother's away so cut school dinner, banking on exams to disturb routine, and went home with her & made ourselves a first rate dinner. So the S Certs over – definetely failed Latin – Not one decent exam. Ah well – will not mention it again until Aug 20th.

END OF SCHOOL CERT.

29
TUESDAY

Two strings burst in my raquet. Absolutely flaming – took it to Gordon Eastons & they replaced them free of charge, but it was pretty thick all the same. Appointed library steward for History section with Jen so started putting files in order and putting the books in order & checking them. Good fun. Did practically nothing but talk all day and do odd jobs. Gets a bit boring after a time but it's a nice change.

30
WEDNESDAY

The day of the eclipse today but so cloudy here that nothing was visible & it only went a little colder and slightly darker. However, listened to radio in half of the eclipse in Sweden & Shetlands. It sounded wonderful. VIth are putting a full scale production of "Comus" by Milton and while crossing hall Miss Cottrell called me and asked me if I knew anything about play, told me to read it paying particular attention to the part of Comus! Perhaps I'm going to understudy Irene Graham. Quite an honour! Watched Drobny & Patty on M's TV. They were superb. Hope Drobny wins final.

JULY
1954

1
THURSDAY
Dominion Day, Canada

Started advanced work today after two days brief respite
So far am taking advanced English, history and French &c
The history promises to be super— Mrs. Merlin for the
English (Tudor Period) and Mrs Blake for the foreign.
The English is Othello, Much Ado about Nothing, Canterbury
Tales, Jane Eyre, A Winters Tale & another book (not
chosen yet). The French stinks. Much to hard for poor me.

2
FRIDAY

Timetable changed already! Am now taking advanced
Latin (heaven help me!) after I've resat it in Nov (;
This is so that I can read history at University. I
Think I want to be a Journalist — get a degree (just
like that!) and take a secretarial course. We go
swimming 2nd period on Friday now. Had a good swim
The play was coarse, I thought, but enjoyed good gossip

3
SATURDAY

Bought some super poplin to make a dress with at
Binns summer sale. Its lime green & grey & white in a
contemporary design. Its super. Went into Binns with
Mum & we had Fruit trifle & I had an iced orange
squash as well. Cut the dress out in evening— Flared
skirt, dolman sleeves (short) and round neck.

4
SUNDAY
3rd after Trinity
Independence Day, U.S.A.

Got on with dress and finished Mary Tudor. It was
a jolly good book, but I have not been able to
skim through it as I usually skim through books

1
THURSDAY

Started advanced work today after two days brief respite! So far am taking advanced English, History and French. The History promises to be super – Mrs Marlin for the English (Tudor Period) and Mrs Blake for the Foreign. The English is Othello, Much Ado about Nothing, Canterbury Tales, Jane Eyre, A Winters Tale & another book (not chosen yet). The French stinks. Much too hard for poor me!

2
FRIDAY

Timetable changed already! Am now taking advanced Latin (heaven help me!) after I've resat it in Nov (!). This is so that I can read History at University. I think I want to be a Journalist – get a degree (just like that!) and take a secretarial course. We go swimming 2nd period on Friday now. Had a good swim. The play was coarse, I thought, but enjoyed good gossip.

3
SATURDAY

Bought some super poplin to make a dress with at Binns summer sale. Its lime green & grey & white in a contemporary design. Its super. Went into Binns with Mum & we had Fruit trifles & I had an iced orange squash as well. Cut the dress out in evening – flared skirt, dolman sleeves (short) and round neck.

4
SUNDAY

Got on with dress and finished "Mary Tudor". It was

a jolly good book, but I have not been able to skim
through it as I usually skim through books.

5
MONDAY

Weather inclined to be showery. Off all day to give
plenty of room in school for Sports & "Comus"
preparations. Did housework in morning and got on
with dress in afternoon – by hand! The dratted machine
broke down (it would when I was in the middle of
making a dress). Suddenly remembered in evening
that we had to have 1st chapter of Ramuntcho read
for tomorrow so had a frantic time racing through it!

6
TUESDAY

Ye Gods! Miss Wynne has begged me to understudy
the part of "Comus"! Excused lessons to learn it and
murmured it all day. At the end of the day I felt I knew
it fairly well. In the afternoon she put me through the
action on the stage and I spouted till I was hoarse! Miss
Cott. interviewed everybody today to decide on subjects.
Mine are History, English and – <u>LATIN</u>! Think det.
to be <u>Journalist</u>.

7
WEDNESDAY

Today was the long excursion day. A bus load of us went
to Clifton potteries – where we had a simply smashing
time watching pottery being made, it was wonderful,
and at the end the potterer said "now who wants a go" so
everyone yelled "Clothy" of course. My goodness! After
6 shapeless masses I turned out what the bus driver said

was a cross between a marmalade jar & an egg cup!
We also went to Lowther Castle & church & had lunch
– 20 Tuna fish sandwiches, ½ lb cheese, 4 choc cream
biscuits and large bottle of pop – by Ullswater. It was
gorgeously sunny. Then we went to Newton Rigg Farm
& trailed 5 <u>miles</u>! Sang all way back! Had a wonderful
day that I'll remember always – with my pot (collected
in 6 wks) as a momento.

Sunny day in cut-down jeans

8
THURSDAY

Sports Day today, and the weather was very kind. Skinny
won The Victrix Ludorum amidst rousing cheers from
us! After the sports was a gym display and dancing.
Then the fair, which was great fun. 2 girls had brought
horses and they were very busy giving rides. Our form
organised Clock Golf & I looked after that most of the
time. It was quite popular. Another form did a ballet-
mime. Another fortune telling. Another super day.

9
FRIDAY

Had to stay for dress rehersal of "Comus". Organised chaos! A bit of scenery collapsed & held up the whole thing. It was 20 to 7 before I finally sneaked out in a dark moment and had a hell of a rush to bolt my tea and dash to the theatre where I collapsed on my bench and just got my breath back before the curtain went up on The Deep Blue Sea. It was wizard. Juno Stevas was the visiting star and she was absol. super.

10
SATURDAY

Spent afternoon & some of evening making my dress. I'm a lazy sewer. What a tussel I had with the back-neck opening – it was like the labours of Hercules! The neck is very plain – high and round – and the whole dress is simple – but not simple enough for me! Had fresh strawberries & icecream for tea – delicious. Thompson won Open Golf.

11
SUNDAY

Went with Shirley & Gordon in afternoon taking colour photographs. Hope they turn out alright. Glorious day – hot and sunny with all sorts of lovely scents in the air.

12
MONDAY

Only had 3 lessons today so had a lovely time wasting our time & talking in the library. Gossiped for five periods all together – about everything & everybody! Finished dress today. Its quite attractive. School Council meeting,

but pretty boring. Only two suggestions. Being bullied
to do something for Mag. Futile!

13
TUESDAY

First performance of Comus today. M & I are the
stage hands and were kept very busy running errands,
closing windows and drawing curtains besides shifting
scenery. The woodland scenery is okay to move but the
Palace Scenes just about kill us! Again, spent a lot of
time in the library & just about came to blows with that
blank blank blank Jennifer Bird. Comus went down
very well and everyone seemed to enjoy it.

14
WEDNESDAY

Played Tennis most of the afternoon. The weather was
most peculiar – raining one minute & hot & sunny the
next. Got Lorna into a fearful paddy & M & I killed
ourselves laughing at her. First evening performance
of Comus tonight. I was a shower-to-seatser and was
kept very busy. Again, it seemed to go down very well –
better than yesterday even I thought. Jennifers French
girl, Francoise, has arrived and is very attractive. The
scenery & costumes of Comus are simply super –
although the sewing is not anything wonderful! Did
something for school mag – description of last Wed!

15
THURSDAY

Copied out thing for mag. Matinee performance of
Comus to other schools. Irene is in the best of health,

so I won't need to do the part. In a way I'm sorry – it's a dogs life being understudy and scene shifter! You see an altogether different aspect of a play. And really, the show couldn't go on without us! Irene prevailed upon me to swim in the Medley. Blasted nuisance.

16
FRIDAY

School swimming sports today. Had to swim in medley – back crawl, which I can't swim for toffee but I managed to give the team about 2 feet lead. Went to Jennifers for tea to meet Francoise her French friend – she's awfully nice. Very attractive in a swarthy way with a lovely smile. We took her to the Theatre and although not understanding much she seemed to enjoy herself very much.

17
SATURDAY

Had an absolutely awful cold – must have resulted from last nights soaking. Mum, Dad & Pud went to Silloth to try & get booked for a weeks holiday and eventually got fixed up in a seemingly delightful new hotel. I stayed at home and went to bed early with this wretched cold.
Had my mop shorn this morning. Awful!

18
SUNDAY

Stayed in bed all day in attempt to get rid of this dreadful cold – partially successful. Passed the time reading poetry – esp. Poems for speaking (Rawnsley).

19
MONDAY

Weather seems to have changed for the better – sunny

and warm though windy today. Hail to good weather! Listened to rehersal of usual Musical Concert. The recorders were awful (not sour grapes!) and I was jolly glad I was not playing with them – never realised that they sounded so awful. Got another historical novel from Mrs Marlin "Man on a Donkey". Started it. Seems quite good.

20
TUESDAY

Ossie beat Curry 6–4, 3–6, 10–8 today in the singles finals. Most thrilling match – it was smashing. The last set was wonderful. Time and time again Ossie lost set point and Curry fought back like a tiger. Shes marvellous. Jolly glad Ossie won through – she had rotten luck last year tearing a ligament in the last set against Pat Jones. I'll lay 100–1 that Audrey Curry wins next year!

21
WEDNESDAY

Doubles finals today, but nothing really startling. Curry and Cameron beat Ossie and Haile in 2 straight sets by 7–5, 6–3. Ossie was off colour today but Mary Haile who was the weakest player of the four, really put up a splendid show. Only lasted about 50 mins. Got out of a lousy lecture on birds by a Mr Eric Hardy to get on with the School Calendar which Miss Cottrell has asked M & I to do. Did the illustrations to it at home and it nearly sent me batty. However, got it finished eventually and it was not to bad. Weather is terrible – rainy, cloudy and cold. What a July!

Breaking up song of Lower School!
2 more hours of woe
2 more hours of sorrow
2 more hours in this old dump
And we'll be free tomorrow!
Sung to: One man went to mow …

22
THURSDAY

Broke up today. Mary Haile is to be our next head girl
and Miss Cottrell had just said Mary Ha– when the
cheers & applause nearly took the roof off. Oh I love the
last assembly – the cheers, the school song, then God
Save the Queen. The tears were streaming down my
cheeks! Then the handing out of reports. The "have-a-
good-holiday" shouts etc etc. Then we all stand at the
corner & furtively open reports & talk!

23
FRIDAY

Went to the Theatre to see: I lived with you. It was very
good & enjoyed it very much but I did not agree with
the ending. Wrote a letter to Gillian, overdue too. Went
to town in afternoon & looked around. Went to library
& got a Bruce Graeme novel. It was quite good but
prefer Berkely Gray. Weather terrible – rain, rain, rain.
Hope it means a really blazing August.

24
SATURDAY

Bought a pair of shorts – white, _very_ short with two
pockets. Super but rather daring! Bought Gill some

scent – Sky High – for her birthday and sent it off. Also a birthday card. Washed mop in evening – ghastly mess! Listened to some of Saturday Night Theatre & it was quite good. Dad has started his hols.

Margaret, right, and Margaret Crosthwaite, in shorts

25
SUNDAY

Went on pleasant walk in the evening through Lowther Browns. It was dull weather, but at least fine & fairly warm. Praying that the weather will pick up.

26
MONDAY

The morning dawned bright & sunny so I donned a thick polo neck, skirt and blazer and went with Dad to Silloth. It was cold and windy by eleven but it was lovely to walk along the shore and feel the sea stinging our faces. By twelve it was raining, so we had to abandon our fishing and went for dinner, which we enjoyed. We got the 2.40 back and went straight to the pictures. It was Danny Kaye. I liked it.

27
TUESDAY

Pouring down today – raining as though it had never rained before. Did housework in morning. Everyone was grumpy with the rain. Finished a book in afternoon & after tea went for a walk along the river and up the spur and through the fields. It was super – a driving wind and lashing rain, almost a gale. Glorius especially high up. I love walking in a storm. Why people shun it I cannot think.

28
WEDNESDAY

This weather is absolutely disgusting – rain & even cold in July! If it doesn't pick up soon we'll be in winter again without having any Summer except for a few miserable days early on. Usual housework in morning. Returned the Library book that Mrs Marlin gave me this afternoon and had a stroll round town. Walked back and saw the river was swollen almost to bursting point & the waterfall is thundering over with tremendous force. Went to City to see "The long, long trailer" and "The Actress". Jean Simmons & Spencer Tracy were super in the Actress. Keep thinking of that School Cert. Not long now. Wish I could sit it again.

28
THURSDAY

Went to theatre tonight. The play was "Dial M for Murder" which was super. I thought the plot was terrific. We all sat along the front row of The Gods & sucked lollipops vigorously. That lousy Peter Evans wasn't playing his tin can tonight. Thank goodness – we'd quite made up our minds to boo him. Weather is still absolutely lousy – cold, rainy & miserable. Hope its nice next week.

30
FRIDAY

Washed a couple of frocks for Silloth. Ironed in afternoon – whopping pile. Had a super strawberry & icecream treat – over a ¼ lb strawberries, wafers and a 3d block of ice cream each. They were scrummy. If only we'd had the weather to go with them. Read a "Woman" in evening & listened to radio. Like winter. Got 10/- from Granda for my holidays. Very gratefully received.

Went to town and bought a pair of white plimsoles to knock around Silloth in and for Tennis. They were just cheap ones (4/6) but they'll do fine for me. Aunty Jean and Uncle Dave arrived about 6.30 on their way back home after their holidays. They'd been to quite a lot of places in the fortnight, but the weather hadn't been VG.

AUGUST
1954

① AUGUST
SUNDAY
7th after Trinity

Went a walk with Shirley & Gordon to Cummersdale by road and back by the river. Very nice. Weather slightly better tho' leaves much to be desired for Aug.

② MONDAY
Bank Holiday—England, Irish Republic, N. Ireland, Scotland

Got a letter from Pu giving train she's coming on. Wrote right away to see if she could switch it as its a dinnertime one & rather inconvenient. Not a bad sort of day. Sunny but rather blustery. Packed in the evening. Knowing Silloth we all packed warm as well as cool clothes! Sewed jeans in afternoon where they had split. Hope weather is glorious!

③ TUESDAY

Arrived at the Inglewood safely. Seems a very nice hotel. Weather sunny but windy. Played tennis with Pud in the afternoon after a swell lunch. Then went for a walk to Skinburness. It was lovely & blowy — The sea was windswept and the sun shone. Took the owners oldest alsation for a long walk after dinner. We stood on the wet sands and gazed across at the sun sinking behind the purple hills — a breathtaking sight.

4 WEDNESDAY

Perfectly glorious day. Up by seven to take Teddy for a walk. It was wonderful out at that time — a slight mist over the sea and a cloudless sky. Went nearly to the point & back then came back and ate a huge breakfast.

1
SUNDAY

Went a walk with Shirley & Gordon to Cummersdale by road and back by the river. Very nice. Weather slightly better tho' leaves much to be desired for Aug.

2
MONDAY

Got a letter from Gill giving train shes coming on. Wrote right away to see if she could switch it as it's a dinnertime one & rather inconvenient. Not a bad sort of day. Sunny but rather blustery. Packed in the evening. Knowing Silloth we all packed warm as well as cool clothes! Sewed jeans in afternoon where they had split. Hope weather is glorius!

3
TUESDAY

Arrived at The Inglewood safely. Seems a very nice hotel. Weather sunny but windy. Played tennis with Pud in the afternoon after a swell lunch. Then went for a walk to Skinburness. It was lovely & blowy – the sea was winswept and the sun shone. Took the owners oldest alsation for a long walk after dinner. We stood on the wet sands and gazed across at the sun sinking behind the purple hills – a breathtaking sight.

4
WEDNESDAY

Perfectly glorious day. Up by seven to take Teddy for a walk. It was wonderful out at that time – a slight mist over the sea and a cloudless sky. Went nearly to the point & back then came back and ate a huge breakfast.

Lay on a deck chair on the sea front with Mum in the morning. It was lovely – the heat was relieved by a breeze from the sea. In the afternoon we went on to the shore & just basked in the sun. Got gloriously sunburned. After dinner went to see the sun set over Criffel. Tommy Trinder came with us & kept us interested with his talk about aeroplanes and stunts. He's a De Haviland man.

5
THURSDAY

Poured down all morning! Went for a walk by the sea shore. It was super. In the afternoon it got out beautifully so donned my jeans and sweater and went for a long, long walk. Round the point and back by the marsh and aerodrome. It was super – seven miles in all. In the evening after a scrumptious dinner (too much to eat at this place) went to the little cinema with Mum & Pud.

6
FRIDAY

Slight shower in the morning but afternoon was lovely. Went for a bathe at West Silloth & we took some snaps. It was smashing in the sea with the sun dancing on the waves. Went to see "Odette" in the evening. A marvellous & deeply moving film. Sat and talked with Trinder & West when we came back over biscuits and tea. It promises to be a lovely day tomorrow – the Trinder is sarcastic about the old saying.

PEOPLE WE MET AT THE INGLEWOOD 1954

Mr & Mrs Wallace

She was small, fat & a cripple. Very old fashioned and wrapped up in her grandchildren. Tolerable. He was tall thin & a semi-invalid. Not much to say but very nice.

Mr & Mrs Conovan

She was large & fat & jolly. Wrapped up in her bowls and library books. A nice person really. He was small and fat with specs on the end of his nose and very brisk.

Mr, Mrs & Master Calcott (only for 2 days)

She was slim & attractive with lovely dark hair. A charming person. He was a rather self important but still pleasant ex-Raf type. The little boy was a rather cocky but quite cheery youngster.

Mr Brian Trinder

Tall, thin chap with a comical face & a covering of curly hair which was rather sparse. Very lively and cheery. 33 with a wife & 2 children. Crazy on women and had a rather nice girl friend! Tommy Trinder, the comedians, cousin. Liked noise & bustle & had the radiogram on whenever he was in. Worked for the De Haviland air company. Hated Silloth – too dull for him. A thorough comic, but very likeable (in small doses).

Mr Mystery Man
Only here for 1 day. Tall, broad, with sun tanned face
& lovely fair hair. Slow charming smile. Wizard! Very
good looking.

Mr L West (Greenways, Buntingford, Herts)
A super chap. About 50, medium height, rather plump
with very sun burned face & greyish hair. Very pleasant
face. Trinders partner and boss. Lovely smile. Married
with 2 children. Awfully jolly & lots of fun. Paid me a
lot of sincere compliments. I will remember him always
as a very nice man.

———————

The owner – Mrs Finlayson
Small, giggly but efficient & pleasant.

Mr Finlayson
Cheery Scots chap. Very affable.

Manageress: Mrs Richardson
Very nice, but didn't see much of her.

The Waitress: Joyce
Bit of a glamour girl but quite nice.

Various others arrived on Saturday but only had first
impressions.

7
SATURDAY

Up by seven & out for a bathe before breakfast. Lovely.
A gloriously hot & sunny day. Sunbathed in afternoon.
Mr T and Mrs G came to visit us & she caught a finger
in a deck chair – horrible. Had tea then sat & talked
with Mr West. Awfully nice chap. Went for a last blow
before getting the 7.23 train.

At the ever popular Silloth

8
SUNDAY

On evening news that Roger Bannister had beaten
Landy with the miraculous time of 3 mins 50 something
in the mile of the century. Also tradgedy of Jim Peters.

9
MONDAY

Lousy weather. Housework in the morning. Gill's bike
arrived safely. Was just getting ready to clean my bike
when Shirley came up with a dress torn to see if I could
mend it as she's hopeless at sewing. Got it mended okay

– but didn't get my chariot cleaned! Gordon brought the snaps which Pud took on holiday but they weren't very good really.

10
TUESDAY

Gave bedroom good clean & put flowers all over the place. Cleaned my bike. Went to meet Gillian on the 5.12. Did not recognise her – high heels, make-up, swagger coat! She looked better when she had a dress & socks on afterwards. She phoned her mother then we went for a walk. I got my feet thoroughly soaked going through a bog. She has no eye for beauty.

11
WEDNESDAY

Set off for Silloth this morning at 10 o'clock. Weather sunny but cloudy & very very windy! Fighting against a flipping gale was exhausting but we enjoyed it all the same. Stopped outside Wigton for an apple and again at Abbey Town for a drink. Went along the shore road (and what a fight) to Silloth! Had a smashing lunch there which Mr West very kindly paid for we found later. West & Trinder were delighted to see us. A fight to reach Alanby but from there we were blown back home. Lovely, but Gill was exhausted & I was sore!

12
THURSDAY

Glorius morning. Gill & I got the train to Keswick where the weather was fresh but cloudy. Rained on the steamer across Derwent to Lodore. The sun came out however as we climbed Cauder Crag and it was beautiful at the top. Breathtaking view. Rained again on way back to Keswick but fared up again & we took a boat out on the lake. Nearly got wrong train at Penrith! Lovely days outing.

13
FRIDAY

Letter from Trinder saying he would be in Carlisle for 2 hrs this morning. Took Gill round shops then met him & went to the Cathedral & Castle, climbing to the top of both. Brought T home for lunch then set him to bus. Afternoon was glorius so we cycled to Gretna Green and took some snaps at the Border line. Glorius cycle back. Went to the pictures in the evening. Lovely clear sky tonight.

14
SATURDAY

Did the castle museum & the castle again today. Cycled to Bowness-on-Solway by the marsh road this afternoon. The weather was lovely on the way but coming back ran into a curtain of rain & got soaked. Went to the theatre (Gordon gave us three seats very nice of him) it was VG.

15
SUNDAY

Went to Hammonds Pond in the evening & Gill & I took a boat out. Went to St. James in the morning.

16
MONDAY

Weather lousy, hellish, awful. Went to the baths in the morning and taught Gill how to swim underwater and how to life save. Had quite a good time in the baths. Weather was still awful in afternoon so spent in writing letters and generally tidying up our "affairs"! Went to the flics in the evening to see "His Majesty O'Keefe". Gill thought it was very good, but didn't fancy it much myself.

17
TUESDAY

Weather still terrible. Went to town in morning and gorged ourselves in Binns. I had a scrumptious meringue glace – meringue, ice, & whipped cream with pineapple. Gill had a fruit sundae then on top of that we had coffee and scrummy cakes – all creamy! Went to Wetheral in afternoon – Got soaked coming back but it was nice there. Went to Rep in evening – super – Birthday Honours – Brenda Sanders super.

18
WEDNESDAY

Rain lashed down today – dead horrible weather and flipping forecast says fine and sunny!! These flipping meteroligists. Just spent the afternoon reading – Gill started "Reach for the Sky" that whizzing book about Douglas Bader the legless pilot. Fared up in evening so went down to bay; it was thundering over & the beck had flooded the path. If we have much more rain the river will flood. Gill set Mums hair while I went for a walk round the Cemetry. Everything was so fresh after the rain.

19
THURSDAY

Rain, rain, rain – nothing but rain. Gill washed her hair

in the morning & spent ages fixing it. Glamour Girl! In
the afternoon went down to the bay with Gordon to take
some photos to try out his new camera – but, of course,
it lashed down and we spent most of the time under a
tree. Smashing tea – <u>tuna fish</u> sandwiches. Sick to death
of pictures but went with Gill to Bochergate. Not bad.

20
FRIDAY

Awake by seven & lay listening to all the gates – every
time one clicked I shot out of bed thinking it was the
postman. Eventually he came but there were no results.
Felt very much relieved! Took Gills bike to station & left
it in luggage office. Then had a last look round town &
bought scrummy gateau! After seeing Gill off I went to
see Genevieve at the "City". It was quite good – but not
as good as they made out. Washed mop and had bath.

21
SATURDAY

Repetition of yesterdays awakening – but again no
luck. Getting on my nerves. I know I've failed Latin
– dammit – & I have my doubts about Eng lang. &
Phys & chem. Letter from Pud saying she was arriving
at 12.20, so went to meet her. Shes had her hair curled
& waved by Grace and it looks quite attractive. Its still
rainy weather!

22
SUNDAY

Went to church with Mum in evening as well as going
in morning – results sure to come tomorrow so prayed
very, very hard, tho' it's a bit late now!

23
MONDAY

8 out of 9 passes

Well, they came! As I knew, I've failed in Latin. Having
duly sworn I was compensated to see some V.G results.
I seem to have got over 80 for English Literature &
Geography & over 70 for History & <u>Science</u>! I think
that's what "Very Good" & "Good" mean. Met various
people & heard their results, but none of our lot. Saw
Pud off in afternoon then went with Mum to get her
a new brolly! See in tonights paper that Colin got only
5 passes.

24
TUESDAY

Went with Mum to Mrs Gillespies – & of course she
had a fool proof excuse for Colin only getting 5 – some
cock & bull story about only concentrating on those he
needed! And he didn't even get Maths. Really! Our
results were in the paper – I'd like to know how many
had straight passes and how many VGs. Some surprises.
I see little Valerie Hepple got 9. I'm still cursing myself!

25
WEDNESDAY

Cut our grass this afternoon. It was quite a nice day
& as the sun was shining it made it very hot work.
Also cut Mrs Harrisons for her. Mum had Mrs G &
Mrs Macphail over to tea, so made tea for them. After
they went Mum went to cut the cemetery grass & put
some flowers on her mothers grave. I followed after

washing the dishes, but I missed her & met Granda. On returning home I found she was still not in – and lo & behold she was still cutting the bally grass on the grave! Dad did garden path.

26
THURSDAY

Lovely day – just as August should be – sunny, hot. Hope it keeps up. In the morning I went to Denton Holme & town for various errands. Saw Mum safely off to Motherwell in afternoon then bought a "Woman" and lazed in deck chair until it was time to make Gordon's tea. Had Dads to make also. European Games are super. Looking forward to Sunday when the 1500 metres is held.

27
FRIDAY

Up bright & early! Got Gordons breakfast ready alright with no complaints. Spent the morning in routine housework then after dinner went to town, changed library book and did some shopping. Discovered some super apples – small, hard as nails & sweet. Must get some more. Am slimming in earnest – almost starvation diet. The theatre was quite good but not my type.

28
SATURDAY

Gordon was in a panic this morning when he found that he had packed all his shirts – so I had to dash down town & buy him one! What a carry on getting him away! Saw Shirley & him of at station – lucky dogs going to Scandanavia. They looked very smart and

excited. Hope Shirley isn't sick – she threatens to be!
Weather nice – then rained!

29
SUNDAY

Listened to thrilling race between Bannister and
Neilson in 1500 metres. Hurrah for Bannister who
won! Big surprise in 5000m – Zatapek was <u>third</u>! Is
there a plot between him & the Russian who won by
<u>100 yds</u>? Chataway 2nd.

30
MONDAY

Got up at 8. Still on my "starvation" diet – orange juice,
apples & maybe a boiled egg or small salad. Had a very
busy morning washing clothes in addition to the usual
household chores. It was a lovely drying day – sunny
with a strong wind – and had clothes dried in no time.
Ironed them in the evening. Then had a rest for a bit
before Dad came.

31
TUESDAY

Felt awfully weak when I got up this morning so I
thought I had better stop the slimming and start eating
solid food. Had diarreoha too. Felt better in afternoon
so walked over to Jeans and had a pleasant time. Stayed
for my tea. Also borrowed "Jane Eyre" which we have to
read in the hols for English. Very busy in the morning
– washed step, grate, bk floor. Raining.

SEPTEMBER
1954

1 SEPTEMBER
WEDNESDAY

Glorious day! Very, very hot & sunny. Usual shift to do in morning & also cleaned all the windows inside & out. In the afternoon I lazed in deck chair for an hour – boiling hot. Then went for my hair appointment at 3.30. I had it parted in the middle, a fringe cut and swept back at the sides. It looks very neat – a change anyway. It cost me 6/- to have it cut, shampooed & set. Treated myself to a tin of Tuna fish & had lovely tea of Tuna sandwiches, orange juice & cake reading T. Eye.

2
THURSDAY

Cloudy at first – then down it came! Still very hot tho! Another note from Mum saying that she's coming back on Saturday evening in Uncle Dave's car. Roll on Saturday! Miss her every minute. I'll never marry & have a family – housekeeping for two is bad enough & only for a week – but for life...! Still no word from Roddy. Dropped Dad's egg on grill so had to give him toast!

3
FRIDAY

Was going to bake but decided to wait until tomorrow. Went uptown in morning and did shopping for weekend. Dad had his dinner in town as he had to go and pay for the carpet – which we got in the afternoon & laid in the evening – so made myself some pancakes. The carpet is a deep red with a pattern on – quite nice. Enjoyed the Theatre immensely – everyone was very gay.

I
WEDNESDAY

Glorius day! Very, very hot & sunny. Usual stuff to do in morning & also cleaned all the windows inside & out. In the afternoon I lazed in deck chair for an hour – boiling hot. Then went for my hair appointment at 3.30. I had it parted in the middle, a fringe cut and swept back at the sides. It looks very neat – a change anyway. It cost me 6/- to have it cut, shampooed & set. Treated myself to a tin of Tuna fish and had lovely tea of Tuna sandwiches, orange juice & cake reading J. Eyre!

2
THURSDAY

Cloudy at first – then down it came! Still very hot tho! Another note from Mum saying that she's coming back on Saturday evening in Uncle Daves car. Roll on Saturday! Miss her every minute. I'll <u>never</u> marry & have a family – housekeeping for two is bad enough & only for a week – but for life …? <u>Still</u> no word from Gordon. Dropped Dads egg on grill so had to give just toast!

3
FRIDAY

Was going to bake but decided to wait until tomorrow. Went up town in morning and did shopping for weekend. Dad had his dinner in town as he had to go and pay for the carpet – which we got in the afternoon & laid in the evening – so made myself some pancakes. The carpet is a deep red with a pattern on – quite nice. Enjoyed the theatre immensely – everyone was very gay!

4
SATURDAY

Got up at 7.30 & had all the housework done by 9.30.
Started baking at 10 and made a chocolate cake, some
buns and & scones (fairly successfully!) Also did
flowers, scrubbed floors, iced cakes & generally got
everything in apple pie order for Mum. Wonderful to
have her back! They arrived at 8.20. Brought me chocs,
Goya bath essence and Goya soap (Pink Mimosa).

5
SUNDAY

Uncle Dave met me out of church & we had a lovely run
round by Welton and Thursby. In afternoon took Mum
& A. Jean round by Burgh Marsh. Very enjoyable.

6
MONDAY

Mum & I got the housework done quickly between us
& then Mum washed – quite a lot to do! Met Pud of
the 4.25 from Nottingham. She had had a marvellous
time there. She says Micky hasn't got his results yet –
poor thing! Phoned A. Nan in evening. Pud has knit a
lovely white ski cap while she was away.

7
TUESDAY

Had a card from M. asking me to meet her in town so
I did. We had a glorius gossip – she about Germany.
She brought me some lovely ladybirds to screw into my
camel coat. In the afternoon I drew £5 out of the bank
(my conscience smiting me!) I bought a wizard checked
skirt & a blue jumper. The skirt is strait with an

inverted pleat back & front. Its blue and green flecked tweed with red over check. <u>Wizard</u>

8
WEDNESDAY

Well – back to school again! Hurrah! The advance set – that's me – is in the library, for a form room with wizard lockers. It's a smashing form room – and there's only 17 of us! I can see the lower VIth year is going to be great fun. Miss Beaumont is our form mistress – jolly decent inspite of wearying lectures of our duties as sixth formers! I was elected Form Captain by the Form & Games representative & School Council. Had a smashing first day at school. Bubbling over with life! Everyone has admired my hair.

9
THURSDAY

Started some work today. Got an essay to be in by a week on Monday for Mrs Marlin. Discussed what one requires in a good novel with that dull old stick Miss Carr in English. Wish we had Polly for English. Polly came up & congratulated me on an excellent Lit result – absolutely <u>gushed</u>. Ugh! Said I was top of all who took it by a long way. Very gratifying!

10
FRIDAY

Bought myself a pen today – an Onoto. It was 10/6. Went to the rep. with my new togs on & they were greatly admired by all. The play was whizzing – just plain funny from beginning to end. We all roared at

Richard Hart – he really is very good and very funny. Have 17 free periods on my timetable but will need them all. Am going to read The Times everyday (!).

11
SATURDAY

Went to town & bought Mums cardigan – it's a lovely limey green (26/-) & myself another jumper – this time in an apple green. Also went to the library. Jen brought my "thing" that I made at Clifton Potteries in July – its peculiar but cute! All my own work too! Gordon returned home – had a marvellous time. Liked Copenhagen best.

12
SUNDAY

Heard all about their holiday today. They brought some cute little candle novelties back – a snowman, two cactus, plum & 2 dice. Really cute!

13
MONDAY

Back to school. Lifes great! Got on with History essay & finished it in the evening. Miss Haigh asked me to say something at the annual [illegible] of Help meeting tomorrow on whether should announce form with highest total or not in case there was a deathly hush when we were asked! Had a bath & composed speech to say – also ran through Rawnsley poem in bath.

14
TUESDAY

MUMS BIRTHDAY – bought a lime green cardigan 26/- (Broke!!)

My little speech was quite effective! Another new girl – Judith Tweddle from the Margaret Sewell. Seems very nice. Had a crazy dancing lesson with the new gym mistress – Miss Ralph. She's broad Lancashire and you cant help laughing at her! She had us doing one of those soppy English country dances pretending we were <u>windmills</u>!!

15
WEDNESDAY

Took some biscuits for Rec. – they didn't last long between M. & I! Have 17 free periods but I could use more. Already we're bound under with dratted Latin – proses, sentences, unseens poetry etc. I <u>loath</u> the dratted subject. History was very interesting though. I like European best – especially wars. I like French History especially. Got plenty to do for History too. Miss Carr is dead feeble for English – & her reading is absolutely void of expression. Feel sorry for her really – she's rather pathetic. Hurricanes still rife over America & great damage has already been done.

16
THURSDAY

M & I had a practise for the Rawnsley in the hall today at 4. M. isn't sure about "Orpheus" but I am about "Horses on the Camargue" by Roy Campbell. Its wizard poetry. Weather dreadful. Got an invitation to Jennifers (Stephenson) birthday party – going to tea then to the theatre. Also get jolly good grub there!! Said on news that there had been a 60 mph gale here today!

17
FRIDAY

The theatre was super & we had a jolly good talk. Got to know today that I have been awarded the Geog. Prize, so spent ages in Thurnams looking for a suitable book – found "Swiss Enchantment" but 12/6 & we are only allowed 8/6. Got my <u>Captains</u> badge today. Newer than ones I've had before. Put my blazer on to go to theatre as it looked nice but it was cold later.

18
SATURDAY

Spent the day mucking about generally. Read "How Green is my Valley" a fairly old novel now but I'd never read it before. It was super. Really <u>credible</u>. Mum got an apron as a present from dad today. Its quite smart! Joan was over this afternoon. She's a cute little thing.

19
SUNDAY

Shirley over – brought Mum a pair of lovely blue towels for her birthday. Shirley's birthday too – Mum gave her a pair of nylons & she got other things too.

20
MONDAY

Miss Beaumont made a mistake – my prize is an Examination Prize & not a Geog. Doesn't seem to be any subject prizes. Our new hearthrug came – it's a lovely thick green one. Mrs Marlin set us a new essay & a book to read. I had the book first & found it very good – Daughter of Time – about whether RIIIrd murdered princes or not. I don't think he did somehow.

21
TUESDAY

Had a tearful Joyce Shakespeare on my hands this morning! She has been told that she is getting a History Prize. She says she doesn't feel she should have it because I was top by a bit in the mock & real thing & I knew everything in class and loved History. Everyone has been saying that evidently & regarded it as a forgone conclusion I would get. Able to comfort her by saying it came naturally to me while she had worked jolly hard. Also, an exam prize covers everything. Windbags should shut up!

22
WEDNESDAY

Davey Wallace came yesterday. He wanted to go out in the evening today so jugged Latin & went. We went for a walk round the Cemetery first then we went to see "The French Line" at the City. It was terrible! Bored stiff! Didn't get home until 10.30. Jane Russel is awful – her mouth is pure ugly & its only her legs that are nice. Grand row at school – we had been having a 3rd music practise for Speech Day & as there was 10 mins left Miss Carey thought it a good idea to have a singsong. While we were singing "One man went to mow" Miss Cottrell stalked onto to the platform & amid deathly silence said "This is scandalous" and sent us back to our formrooms! Miss Carey didn't know what to do! Talking point!

23
THURSDAY

Got our History essays back from Mrs Marlin. I got
A – and she said the essay I did – "Explain why H
VII became King in 1485" – was the one requiring
most thought. Everyone else got B's or B- or B+ (2).
Vivien was furious because she had written 13 sides!
I only wrote 6. Jolly pleased. David went away today
to Blackpool (of all stinking places!). He has some
whizzing looking golf clubs with him.

24
FRIDAY

The theatre was very good, I thought. It was a french
comedy – "The Little Hut" – translated into English.
It was rather obscene, but when it is funny that can be
forgiven. Had to take form business today & dropped
the flipping dinner register in some ink – so we all had
a high old time trying to rub it off! Harvest Festival
at School today – not half as good as usual due to bad
summer I expect.

25
SATURDAY

Rawnsley trials this morning. Joan Atkinson is good
but rather emotional when reading prose; Elizabeth
Atkinson is stolid; Jennifer Lees is jolly good only a
bit quick. I think M & I stand quite a good chance.
I love my poem. If only I can go slowly when reading
I shouldn't do so badly. If only!

26
SUNDAY

Shirley wanted to go for a walk this evening so Gordon & I walked her to Cumersdale via the river path. Was she sickened! We missed the bus & had to walk home.

27
MONDAY

Well, Rawnsley is over. Elizabeth Richardson won! Much to everyone's shock & surprise. She was very correct but I think M. should have won hands down. M was runner up. I thought, after hearing everyone, that M. would win & I might be runner up. My poem got the biggest clap but my reading was <u>far</u> too quick! M's reading was really excellent. Fancy E. winning. Miss C. said we were all ex etc etc and very dif. to pick any out.

28
TUESDAY

Practise today down at Central Hall for Speech Day. Usual palaver. We had a ¼ hr. break so we tore to the Dinky Café & had a quick coffee & biscuits. It was a glorious morning – nippy & misty but sunny with a perfectly blue sky. Its really Autumn now. The trees are turning beautiful yellows and browns and reds and the leaves are falling rapidly. I love Autumn!

29
WEDNESDAY

Did such a soppy thing today! I was listening to Mrs. Blake in History with great boredom (what a bore & muddle she is as a teacher, although a charming person)

and absentmindedly twirling my gym girdle round &
round the chair leg in knots. When Mrs. Blake asked
me to close some windows I clean forgot & dragged the
chair with me! You should have heard the roars!! The
plays started again tonight. There was a very good one
on – "From information received". It is going to be a
series of thrillers this time. Again a lovely crisp autumn
day tho rain in the night.

30
THURSDAY

Speech Day today. Got "Mediterranean Blue" for my
prize. It's a lovely book. Also got my cert – very impres-
sive (!). A Miss Joachim from St. Hilds, Durham was
the presenter of prizes. A nice voice but a wandering
speech. Miss Cottrell's wasn't half as clear & concise
& compact as Miss Wilsons report was. And the dress
she had on!! Announced we are going to start building
science labs & dining room. Might be finished by 1964!

OCTOBER
1954

1 OCTOBER
FRIDAY

Got down to some real work in last 2 periods and did English essay — character sketch of Mr. Rochester from Jane Eyre. Play was very good indeed — Someone Waiting — and Richard that was super. Bud went to spend the night with Joan — they're going to Blackpool very early tomorrow & she's staying at Joan's Sat. too — Good oh! I'll have bed to myself.

2
SATURDAY

Have a shocking cold. Did history essay — How did H.VII deal with problem of overmighty subject — in afternoon. Beginning to like the Tudors very much. Worked my map inspite of cold ∴ it was really cluny. It looks dreadful when worked anew! Had a cosy evening with Mum & heard half of play on Sat night Theatre.

3
SUNDAY
16th after Trinity

Went to church in morning but went to bed on return after dinner as cold dreadful. Sore throat as well. Nothing worse than the common cold. O for a cure!

4
MONDAY

Got A (-) for my English of the lake. Hty host — evid. A bracket minus is one degree higher than A minus! Worked hard again today. Copied essays into neat. Cold still foul though throat better. Everyone seems to be similarly afflicted — though that's small comfort! Talked for ages at corner (inspite of cold!) to Jennifer Rose & Maureen Kilby & M. & M. Bewley.

1
FRIDAY

Got down to some real work in last 2 periods and did English essay – character sketch of Mr Rochester from Jane Eyre. Play was very good indeed – Someone waiting – and Richard Hart was super. Pud went to spend the night with Joan – they're going to Blackpool very early tomorrow & shes staying at Joans Sat. too – Good oh! I'll have bed to myself.

2
SATURDAY

Have a shocking cold. Did History essay – How did H VII deal with problem of overmighty subject – in afternoon. Beginning to like the Tudors very much. Washed my mop inspite of cold because it was really dirty. It looks dreadful when washed anew! Had a cosy evening with Mum & heard half of play on Sat night theatre.

3
SUNDAY

Went to church in morning but went to bed on return after dinner as cold dreadful. Sore throat as well. Nothing worse than the common cold. O for a cure!

4
MONDAY

Got A(-) for my English. Highest – evid. A bracket minus is one degree higher than A minus! Worked hard again today. Copied essays into neat. Cold still foul though throat better. Everyone seems to be similarly afflicted – though that's small comfort! Talked for ages at corner (inspite of cold!) to Jenifer Done & Mavis Kilby & M. & M. Bewley.

5
TUESDAY

Seem to have had a busy time today with one thing and another. Jennifer handed on "Dicken" to me – the story of Richard III. It's very good indeed. My cold is dreadful & I have an awful cough to go with it now. Mrs G was over. She says Colin is getting on okay at the Art School. LVI training college are having a Halloween Party for their Barnardo effort – hope that its good!

6
WEDNESDAY

Latin, Latin, Latin – seem to have nothing but Latin on a Wednesday! Start off with a double period of it – too gloomy for words. It'll be the biggest laugh if I fail again in November! I wont be able to face Mrs Andrew – she's expecting me to get a good mark. Got E for my home exercise again! Heigh ho – what have I done to deserve this?! My cold is worse, my nose is really sore round the nostrils with constantly blowing it & my cough it really hollow! What a gloomy paragraph! The play was very good – Holiday in Berlin – The series is excellent – really worth listening too.

7
THURSDAY

Puzzled over that damned Latin Unseen for 1½ hr tonight – and that's the second try at that. At length light dawned & I was able to get some sense out of the beastly thing – although it still sounds pretty garbled! Had a super History lesson with Mrs. Marlin – we just sat & looked at pictures of Florence &

Venice. She said it would give us a gd background for
Rennaisance anyway!

8
FRIDAY

Jennifers Birthday tomorrow so she took 6 of us to the
Lonsdale and then home. M. & I nearly killed ourselves
laughing when we found we were in the 1/9's!! We had a
horrible savoury pie at her house too – but otherwise we
had a super time. The film wasn't too bad – Elephant
Walk – & we had a gd chat at her house til 10.20. Took
some salmon sandwiches to the flics – lovely! Got A on
essay abt. Mr R in J Eyre.

9
SATURDAY

My cold is still with me. Went to the Art Exibition in
the afternoon. There was some very good stuff there – I
particularly liked an oil called "The Tired Workers"
& some birds in flight by a T. Davidson. Listened to
some of play but it wasn't very good. Lovely morning
but turned horrible.

10
SUNDAY

Spent afternoon making Rota for Biscuit Stall at School
(form Barnado Effort) & placards of sort of biscuits
we're going to sell. Ellen over.

11
MONDAY

Got 3 weeks work for History and handed in essay.
English painful as usual – Miss Carr is absolutely
pathetic. Not a lively spark in her. Yet she is very nice really

– just so pitiful. I expect there is "hidden depths" in her tho! Her eyes show she probably is a judge of character & isn't so quiet if you knew her well. Typically school-marmish tho. Poor devil. Probably quite happy tho.

12
TUESDAY

Pud at last was persuaded to take her septic thumb to the Doctors – and he lanced it in a minute! All that fuss for 10 days and it could have been cured ages ago! Mum phoned Aunty Nan to see if she was going into Hospital tomorrow but she isn't. Mike has a sty & is thoroughly browned off with life – poor Micky!

13
WEDNESDAY

My legs are literally <u>killing</u> me! That dancing lesson yesterday nearly killed me – doing those chezoslovakian dances. Miss Ralph the new gym mistress is a scream! Broad Lancashire. Did latin for a double period this afternoon – it beats me. I loath – but you've heard that story before! What'll happen if I fail in Nov. doesn't bear thinking about! Very cold today & extremely blustery – the leaves are nearly all of the trees. Came home by the bay & it was thundering over with the wind whipping huge waves up. I walked through the leaves up the hill & they made the most gorgeous noise – lovely colours too!

14
THURSDAY

The first XI gave North Shields a whacking tonight! Mum didn't go to the theatre tonight as usual – Mrs.

G cant go so they are going tomorrow. Good old Chris Chataway! He set up a new world record yesterday & beat that Russian Zuc [Kuts]! Whizzo! The papers are full of it. Gives a bit of prestige back anyway. Bet he's feeling very proud.

15
FRIDAY

Went to the theatre as usual – I had heard half of it on Sat. Night Theatre so was interested to see what happened in the end. Jennifer S. had her lipstick on tonight – it didn't look bad but I loath that muck & stuff. Mary Wills & Jennifer B. had high heels on & looked dreadful. They looked about 20. Give me socks, flat heels, no makeup & teenage clothes any day! Sods.

16
SATURDAY

Went with Mum to buy her a new coat – about time too as she hasn't had a new winter coat for literally years – 4 yrs. We got a very nice one – rusty red & black flecked tweed with large patch pockets inverted pleat right up back, big collar & lapels & belt. Jolly smart. Also a small black hat which she suits.

17
SUNDAY

Church as usual. Weather dreadful – windy & rain. Got on with "Bleak House" – am determined to fulfil vow to read all Dickens. No hardship – Dickens is wizard.

18
MONDAY

Weather again shocking. Rain all night. Caldew has

burst its banks and the Eden is a torrent. Worse in other places. Miserable in Huts where we have Latin – they are a disgrace to school. Devoted evening to reading "Rennaisance & Reformation" by Green. Its jolly good.

19
TUESDAY

Weather still bad. The Eden is still 2 feet above normal level & the flooding has been very bad. Lower Cumersdale is flooded out & they have been evacuated to upper Cumersdale. Thurstonfield is threatened too. It's a terrible thing to have happened so early in the year especially after such a dreadfully bad summer. Had UIVths as usual today – they spoil me!

20
WEDNESDAY

Floods receeded a bit. Paragraph or so in papers about it – seemingly Wigton was marooned for 24 hrs. It got out quite nice later on tho much colder now. Mum washed sitting room curtains today – they look lovely & fresh. Mugged away at Latin this afternoon – sat beside Mary Haile. She's wizard! I'd rather take Advanced Latin than Ordinary I think – at least you have set books. I'm going to pass Advanced Latin if it's the last thing I do – but I doubt I'll fail Ordinary again!

21
THURSDAY

School Council meeting on Wednesday – I'll have an awful rush that night because of the Halloween Party. Most of our forms going – it's the Lower VI Barnardo effort. Our Tuck shop is going fine & we are beginning to make a jolly good profit. We are adopting another child now because Jimmy is getting to old to belong to a girls school. Maybe a coloured one.

22
FRIDAY

Well, tonight was the last night of this seasons repertory. It was okay but a bit silly – "The Happy Marriage". I'll miss going to the theatre every Friday very much – we've had lots of fun there. I wish I lived in London because then I could go & see all the plays with the really good actors & actresses in them. Here's to next year!

23
SATURDAY

Got my hair cut & washed it in the evening. I have decided to wash it every Friday night now instead of once a fortnight. Am reading the life story of the Brontës at present – don't seem to have read a really trashy good book for ages. No time for Denis Wheatley and Berkerly Gray now!

Her mop under control

24
SUNDAY

Usual Sunday routine. Cold & damp at first but got out very nice in the afternoon. Wrote to Gillian at last – don't seem to have time to write long letters now.

25
MONDAY

Writing this while "Top of the Form" is just finishing. It is a jolly good series & this one was very good. Wish our school took part in it – it would be fun – or would it?! Did History essay this evening. Have decided to take Scholarship English & History. We all have to eat something of everything at school dinners now – gosh! Wait until its dear semolina!!

26
TUESDAY

Went to see a French play at The Creighton – a touring company of French actors who do plays at schools. Saw them do "Le bourgeois Gentilhomme" last year. Didn't think much of it! This year it was "Le Malade Imaginaire". It was a lot better – one bloke was a scream, he played the judges baby son. Didn't understand much of it but enough to get the gist. Cant stick Molièrs plays – soft.

27
WEDNESDAY

It was the LVI Halloween Party tonight – it was wizard. They had made it look marvellous – drawings of witches etc round the room, turnip lanterns to light it, spiders webs across the corners, & some of them dressed up as witches. We had a wizard supper – hot

sausages on sticks, hot potatoes, cakes biscuits etc.
Miss Baxter told a ghost story – she had a black dress
on and a witch seated on either side & what with the
flickering light of the room & the rain & wind on the
windows it was really eiry! We had dancing & games &
ducking for apples & charades & biting apples hanging
on string. It was really super! We walked home after a
cup of tea (just a few of us) & didn't get home till 10.10.

28
THURSDAY

Dog tired after last night! My legs are aching like
anything. We had a musical "concert" this afternoon
– it was sheer agony – not the music but our "seats."
We were so squashed that we couldn't get our hands
together to clap! Never again! Pat, Joyce & I went to
The Lakeland Laundry to see if they would take us
for Xmas Hols. But they didn't know so we went to the
Steam – I got engaged! Smashing! (Hard work tho!)

29
FRIDAY

Went to town this morning (half term) and got Mrs
Gaskells "Life of Charlotte Brontë" at the library –
also got 1,000 paper bags for cheese crisps for biscuit
stall. Went for a blow early afternoon – the river is over
again. Spent rest of afternoon doing notes on John &
S Cabot, & Colet for History. Washed the mop with a
"White Rain" Shampoo and got on with "Thomas
More". Quite a decent biography.

30
SATURDAY

Went for a walk in the morning – or rather, dinnertime. Read "More" and finished him in the afternoon and got on with "Wolsey". It's a stinking biography – Pollard writes such complicated books. Finished "Wolsey" in the evening – Thank goodness! Read a bit of Mrs Gaskell's Life of Charlotte Brontë – its quite interesting – better than Pollard.

31
SUNDAY

Had a good brisk walk over to Church. A sunny but nippy morning. Shirley has bought a new umberella – its red with a nice handle & very long as is fashionable.

NOVEMBER
1954

1
MONDAY

Pud suddenly (& most unusually!) decided to do all the housework this morning so I went for a walk right up this side of the river, across the Cunerdale bridge & back on the other side to the waterfowl. I thoroughly enjoyed it — it was a lovely morning. Did notes with Flote in afternoon. Listened to repeat of Wednesday night theatre — it was very good — then did European Notes.

2
TUESDAY
Election Day, U.S.A.

Pud & Mum & I soon got through the housework so Pud & I went to town. It was a lovely morning. We went to the library first & I nabbed a copy of Wolsey in prep. for essay. We also had a grand time browsing over Xmas cards & got a few nice ones. Did Vergil most of afternoon, read in evening. Mum went to Mrs. Gillespies.

3
WEDNESDAY

Nice to get back to school once more. M. had had a good time at Kirkoswald. Everyone is teasing me about going to work in the laundry — not that I care! We had a grand scale Vergil test today! The first 2 periods we were tested on translation syntax & the period at the end of the morning in context & a general question. It wasn't so bad we did it on large foolscap sheets so that it was almost like an exam! Mrs. B a scream! Did a rough draft of "Comus" for school mag. The play was by Somerset Maughan's — "The Lady Frederick" Not b

1
MONDAY

Pud suddenly (& most unusually!) decided to do all the housework this morning so I went for a walk right up this side of the river, across the Cumersdale bridge & back on the other side to the Waterfall. I thoroughly enjoyed it – it was a lovely morning. Did notes on Thom. More in afternoon. Listened to repeat of Wednesday night theatre – it was very good – then did European Notes.

2
TUESDAY

Pud & Mum & I soon got through the housework so Pud & I went to town. It was a lovely morning. We went to the library first & I nabbed a copy of Wolsey in prep. for essay. We also had a grand time browsing over Xmas cards & got a few nice ones. Did Vergil most of afternoon and read in evening. Mum went to Mrs. Gillespies.

3
WEDNESDAY

Nice to get back to school once more. M. had had a good time at Kirkoswald. Everyone is teasing me about going to work in the laundry – not that I care! We had a grand scale Vergil test today! The first 2 periods we were tested on translation & syntax & the period at the end of the morning on context and a general question. It wasn't so bad. We did it on large foolscap sheets so that it was almost like an exam! Mrs. A's a scream! Did a rough draft of "Comus" for school mag. The play was one of Somerset Maughan's – "The Lady Frederick". Not bad.

4
THURSDAY

Got our Vergil tests back – I was top with 75%! It's the only part of Latin I can do or like – pity I wasn't as good at the other things. Had a lovely roaring fire on in the library – it was cold & wet outside. Miss Carr told us today that the school is going to do a play – "The Snow Queen" & wants M & I to go to the auditions tomorrow night. If it's the same as the fairy tale ......!

5
FRIDAY

Went to the "Snow Queen" Audition. There were crowds there so they just had a quick run through of voices. I had to read the part of the Storyteller which I wouldn't mind doing at all, at all! Its very juvenile but perhaps it wont be so bad when it gets going. Dad & Pud bought some fireworks & had a fine time letting them off around a bonfire of rubbish! Washed the mop.

6
SATURDAY

Went to town in the morning. Saw a lovely half slip in Richards & lots of other nice things. I'm having a fine time "shopping" with the money I'am going to earn at the laundry! Joan was here. Floods are awful in the north east & there is snow on the Lake District peaks already. Read "Flush" by Virginia Woolf.

7
SUNDAY

Lovely, lovely morning! Very frosty but sunny. Oh for a holiday in the Autumn spent beside the sea or in the depths of the Lake District! Someday, perhaps.

8
MONDAY

A rainy, cold, miserable Monday. Everyone in a thoroughly beastly mood & as a result there was constant bickering & arguing all day. I decided I <u>loathed</u> Vivien Stewart, she's so smug, jealous & hysterical. On most days I can see her advantages but today I hated her. And I could have hit Valerie & strangled Lorna quite cheerfully. Little prigs. After a thoroughly vicious afternoon cheered up!

9
TUESDAY

A lovely morning after such a stormy yesterday. We got our first essays back from Mrs. Blake – Ye Gods! Were we squashed! She's written <u>screeds</u> on mine! I can hardly read my own writing for red ink, & the others were the same. Viv, Judith & I all got B – what a mock! Lowest I've ever had for an essay! Jen went off the rails & got C-, Win C+ & Doreen B-. Wrote "<u>something</u>" for school mag.

10
WEDNESDAY

Am reading "Orlando" by Virginia Woolf. It's really most peculiar – a sort of biography of a person who lived through 3½ centuries and during that time changed from a man to a woman! Its all very confusing & I don't know that I thought it was very well done, but then I probably can't appreciate it. Great to do about the penalty the Russian referee didn't give during the Arsenal V. Spartak football match! Got beat 2–1 worse luck. It very well looked like a penalty from the pictures in the paper. The play was very good – "The Circle" – by S Maughamn. It was very funny – or rather, witty – in parts.

11
THURSDAY

Our History lesson degenerated into a discussion of detective novels somehow! In Eng. History we looked at Art books. Jen & I poured over a beautiful edition of Michael Angelo's sculptures etc. They're marvellous, wonderful, terrific! It was a dreadful morning & evening but a lovely afternoon in between showers. I love this changeable weather.

12
FRIDAY

Borrowed a "Woman" from M. & had a nice lazy evening by the fire reading it. I find that the stories bore me to death now – it must be with reading so many "good" books! Didn't wash my hair as I'm not getting it cut till Monday and it doesn't cut so well if its just been washed. Joan & Mary are still sitting Cambridge entrance exams!

13
SATURDAY

Spent the afternoon trailing round town with Mum looking for a shade for the standard lamp – without success, we just couldn't find what we wanted. Started on Wolsey essay in the evening – its an awful thing & we've got the Luther one to do for European History as well. What a life! Windy & rainy today.

14
SUNDAY

A truly lovely morning. Took Ellen home & visited

Aunty Ella and co – all very well. Lost one of the ladybirds Margaret brought me from Germany – damn!

15
MONDAY

Got my hair cut at the co-op in Denton Holme – it's a one man – or rather, one woman – affair, but she did it very well. It's a shockingly difference in price – she only charged 1/- while Binn's charge 2/- or even 2/6! Looks as though I'm going to have that acting article published in mag. as well. Got Wolsey off my chest – although I can't imagine what mark I'll get for it! I think he's awful.

16
TUESDAY

Had to stay behind with M. for "The Snow Queen" thing – we only had to read a bit, then we went. Read a lot of "Charles V" by Karl Brandi – jolly heavy going. School Certificate resits start tomorrow; Latin is on Monday – I bet I fail! Wolverhampton Wanderers beat Spartak 4–0! It was terribly exciting – coming right on top of us winning the World Rugby Cup, too. We're coming on!

17
WEDNESDAY

Jennifer forgot she had a History lesson 6th period today. It was killing – half way through the lesson we suddenly realised she wasn't there! But we thought she must be sitting an exam, although I was jolly sure she wasn't. Anyway, when we got back to the library, there she was, sitting quite innocently! How we roared – Mrs Blake too! The play was very good – For Services Rendered, S W Maughn. I like his plays very much. Talked for ages at the corner – although we got colder & colder! The lengths we go to for a good old gossip! Amazing.

18
THURSDAY

Mrs Shaw presented 2 trees to the school today & came herself to plant them, starting a new row on the left side of the hockey pitches – a lilac and a cherry. The VIth form and Form Prefects watched. Did last Novembers Latin paper in Latin today, & disgraced myself thoroughly! I'm hopeless. I had what M. calls a "Latin Complex" for the rest of the day.

19
FRIDAY

Washed the mop and parted it in the middle again (have had it at the side for 4 days). Got the library ready for the exam on Monday – cleared tables etc. & put 9 desks in, put curtain across the window and notices – SILENCE – outside. Looks awful! Mary Haile & Joan Scott are sitting their Oxford entrance in with us.

20
SATURDAY

Spent the morning browsing around the patterns in Binn's – I am crazy to have a turquoise felt skirt with black ric-rac round at intervals, also a new sleeveless blouse and a pair of flat white ballet shoes – all for the Xmas party at school. I expect I'll have to succumb to nylons because of the shoes – but never to make-up.

21
SUNDAY

Cold rainy miserable sort of weather. Did some more swotting for Latin – but it won't be any good! Had a lovely warm bath – nothing better for relaxing.

22
MONDAY

Well, the jolly old exam is over! The first paper was putrid – I made the most glorius hash of the sentences & prose. The first translation I got almost all correct but the second I missed the sense! The second paper wasn't so bad – I could make a pretty good guess at them, anyway. I think I'm just on the borderline. Haunted by fear that I didnt number the questions!

23
TUESDAY

Had the most queer experience today! Got a book on Luther out of the library & when I began my prep I flicked through it & came across a glossy picture of Luther dressed in black, with a beard and a title "Junker Georg". I then wrote a bit of my essay then picked up the book again to look at the picture – and there wasn't one!! There wasn't even a glossy page. I was dumbfounded. I'm sure it wasn't in another book.

24
WEDNESDAY

Called in with M. at Gray's after school. She spent 17/3 on 2 presents, 2 birthday cards & some Xmas cards. I hadn't any cash on me, but Jennifer lent me 3/- & I bought some cards & wrapping paper. The paper is

most unusual – red & white stripped, and also blue &
white. The cards are lovely – but jolly expensive – 2 at
11d each & one at 7d (not so bad). Finished of History
Essay. Lets hope I get a better mark & can see my own
writing when I get it back! The play – another Somerset
Maughan – called "Sheppey" was quite good. It had a
religious theme running through it.

25
THURSDAY

Had the first proper rehearsal for the "Snow Queen"
today. I'm the Snow Queen! – They've cut the Storyteller
out which was a mad thing to do. I'd <u>love</u> to bleach my
hair for the part, but I guess white powder & sparkly
stuff will have to do. Hope I have a decent costume. M.
is the Chancellor. It's a very <u>juvenile</u> sort of play.

The Snow Queen – Margaret at the very back,
Margaret Crosthwaite, in top hat, in front of her

26
FRIDAY

The biscuit stall is getting on fine – we've made over £5 profit all ready. Gets a bit irksome, tho, counting 26 of those small cheese crisps into a bag! But at 2d a bag they go like lightning. Mum has a beastly boil on her left eyebrow – its ghastly. Washed the mop with a "Sunsilk" shampoo this week – I think I've just about tried the lot now! I like "White rain".

27
SATURDAY

Went to town in the afternoon. Saw a lovely bluey turquoise wool dress in Richards which I'd love, but its £4.9.6. Also a wizard waist slip. I'd like a pair of black ballet shoes too. I'm going to have <u>something</u> new for the school party anyhow. I saw a lovely tweedy skirt & a white zip up too!

28
SUNDAY

There was a real storm last night. The wind howled and the rain lashed something awful. I'd have loved to have been out in it. The hall was "flooded".

29
MONDAY

The rehearsal was pretty boring. Miss Wynne really is the giddy limit with her cutting. The damn play is slashed to bits – surely the author knew better than this old battleaxe. Eng. aren't doing very well in the Tests in Australia – it would be dreadful if we lost the ashes again. Some of the critics seem to think the

odds are on the Aussies winning. We've got injuries
in the team too.

30
TUESDAY

Today is Winston Churchills 80th birthday. What
a grand old fellow he is! Those rotten socialists are
stinking – fancy refusing to sign his birthday book!
Bessie Braddock wants thrown in the Thames. Went
to dentist – had Farmer, hes <u>wizard</u>. Got A for History
Essay. Mrs. M. was almost gushing about it! Bucks
one up. (Scholarship one too).

DECEMBER
1954

1 DECEMBER
WEDNESDAY

The play was very good - The moon ⊙ 6° - ⊙ ☽ hated yet sympathised with Strickland. The play rehearsal was lousy - Miss Wynne had left it to the two stooges so it was feeble, to say the least. Neither of them have any spirit at all - especially Miss Cau! Both are completely subservient to that bloated elephant. Started making notes on Cathrine de Medici - she's a jolly interesting person. We beat the Bernard's at football & old Matthews fairly gave them something to think about! Latin was stinking today - none of us could do the ghostly unseen - nettled Mrs A, I'm sure!

2
THURSDAY

Vivien handed over the Biography of Margaret of Austria. Its wizard - after "Charles V" I can simply romp through it! "William the silent" sounds good, too. Went to the dentists again for one filling - it wasn't bad at all - & Mr Fawter was super. He's just like an overgrown schoolboy! Had pancakes for tea - lovely! Latin unseen for prep wasn't bad at all.

3
FRIDAY

Went to the old Girls Guild meeting tonight. It was killing at first - we had to pray after being introduced to the oldest member, who looked about 100, & the secretary. It wasn't so bad later on though - & we had some quite decent games, if rather tuite. The supper was pretty good too - plenty of squashy cream cakes & some sausage rolls. Mum bought me a super red & white spotted scarf today.

1
WEDNESDAY

The play was very good – The moon & 6d. – & I hated
yet sympathised with Strickland. The play rehearsal
was lousy – Miss Wynne had left it to the two stooges
so it was feeble, to say the least. Neither of them have
any spirit at all – especially Miss Carr! Both are
completely subservient to that bloated elephant. Started
making notes on Cathrine de Medici – she's a jolly
interesting person. We beat the Germans at football
& old Matthews fairly gave them something to think
about! Latin was stinking today – none of us could do
the ghastly unseen – neither could Mrs. A, I'm sure!!

2
THURSDAY

Vivien handed over the Biography of Margaret of
Austria. Its wizard – after "Charles V" I can simply
romp through it! "William the Silent" sounds good,
too. Went to the dentists again for one filling – it wasn't
bad at all – and Mr Farmer was super. He's just like an
overgrown schoolboy! Had pancakes for tea – lovely!
Latin unseen for prep. wasn't bad at all.

3
FRIDAY

Went to the old Girls Guild meeting tonight. It was
killing at first – we had to <u>pray</u> after being introduced
to the oldest member, who looked about 100, & the
secretary. It wasn't so bad later on though – & we had
some quite decent games, if rather trite. The supper
was pretty good too – plenty of squashy cream cakes

& some sausage rolls. Mum bought me a super red &
white spotted scarf today.

4
SATURDAY

Had a shopping spree today. Borrowed £4 off Dad.
Bought a pair of super black ballerina shoes 42/6 & Mum
(xmas pres.) bought me a <u>wizard</u> waist slip – very full,
in three divisions with broderie anglais on the bottom
& pink bows on. I also got Dads Xmas present – a silver
medallion belt. We had a super tea in Binns afterwards.

5
SUNDAY

Shirley came up before dinner & stayed to 8 for dinner.
Finished "Margaret of Austria" which I enjoyed very
much – certainly very light after that beastly heavy
Charles V.

6
MONDAY

They were trying out 'Kays' at the play rehearsal so
I had to do one scene with three different kids which
was rather boring. Latin was awful – got practically
nothing right in the beastly prose! Top of the Form was
very good – but again there were some very unequal
questions. Had netball with little Miss Ralph, it wasn't
such a good game as we have with Miss T.

7
TUESDAY

Much colder day & very frosty & foggy at first. Bitterly
cold going down on bike. Joan Scott got to know that
she has got an interview tomorrow at [Cambridge

deleted] Oxford!! She's on top of the world (it gives me a thrill just to write the name – Cambridge!) But poor old Mary hasn't heard anything – I think shes wizard. Tried out for readings for the nativity play. Had amusing dinnertime with my table of UIVs. Look forward to Tuesday.

8
WEDNESDAY

Had a concert this afternoon – a cellist & a pianist. It was sheer agony – we were all crammed on the Hall floor and by the end absolutely sore & miserable. Miss Carr is suddenly dead pally! She invited us to see some slides a bit ago, of her holiday which she spent motoring through Germany, Switzerland, Italy and France, but could not get a room in school to show the film so she invited us home. She lives in one room in Warwick road. Rather bare. We had tea & biscuits & saw the slides which were very good. Poor thing – she was so nervous and so pleased when we liked her slides.

Play was awful.

9
THURSDAY

School Council tonight. Decided: to shout Hurray and not Hurrah: to see what the UIVths think about reviving the old Play Competition; to see about a school 'bus for the baths; to order house badges again & other smaller business. Mum bought me a pair of nylons today – Ugh! But socks look a little silly with flat ballet shoes, so I guess I'll have to succumb to wearing them.

10
FRIDAY

Had a browse round the shops with M. after school. We had to stay for a rehearsal for the "Nativity Ode" first – M., Joan Atkinson & I are saying that Milton between carols. They are having poems & carols & a still scene this year instead of the usual Nativity Play. Copied my History essay – The Pilgrimage of Grace Thing – into neat. Have all those library books to check – don't know when I'll get them done.

11
SATURDAY

Went to town in the morning searching for a dress for the school party, but couldn't find one. Went up again in afternoon & bought some gorgeous tan coloured poplin & some deep turquoise rick-rack to trim it with. Its wizard. Cut it out then sewed most of the evening. Washed the mop. Going to have an awful rush one way & another this week.

12
SUNDAY

Got on with dress. Went to St. James instead of St. Barnabas' because it was pouring. Think I'll start going to St. James – its a lovely old church.

13
MONDAY

Jennifer off, so had Judith & Doreen to help me check the History books. Had to stay & practise The Nativity Ode by Milton with Joan Atkinson & M. We look like the three stooges! Got on with my dress – it is beginning to look very nice. I adore the colour – it's a sort of tangerine shade; the turquoise ric-rac looks most effective.

14
TUESDAY

Jennifer back today, so gave her the luscious job of going through the missing History books to see if she could find any – she's jolly good at that sort of thing. Have collected 7/6 for Miss Beaumonts Xmas present, which isn't bad. We're thinking of getting her a "Peter Scott" or Vernon Ward picture – I should think it would please her.

15
WEDNESDAY

Finished making up the list of missing History books – seems to be an awful lot, but I expect lots of them will turn up when we clear up at the end of term. Went down to the cloakroom on the pretext of washing my hands to see the dresses. They looked very nice indeed – especially Shiela Mason who had made hers herself. Her hair was a mess, tho! So combed it as best I could for her. Finished my own dress today. Listened to the play as I sewed – it was quite amusing really – "The Nutmeg Tree". Not bad.

16
THURSDAY

Finished off my dress & pressed it – the result is highly satisfactory except for a few things! Did no work again today – luscious! Got our essays back from Mrs. Marlin & I got A and she said it was a very nice essay. Everyone is just sitting talking in the library round my lovely fire

– except poor old Norma Marples who vainly asks for
silence to work.

17
FRIDAY

School party today. Had a super dancing display by
Lower IV Q this morning, for their Barnardo effort.
They were all dressed up in national costume. The
Party was wizard – although a bit of a strain! I had a
lot of complements about my dress – it certainly looked
nice. M. looked nice too. Did my bit entertaining the
staff & dancing with them okay!

18
SATURDAY

Slept in until 11 this morning then got up & finished
dusting etc. Went to town to finish my Xmas shopping.
Got a Yardley shaving bowl for Gordon & a cellophane
box of bon bons for Shirley. Got Mum a lovely picture
of 2 foals – a painting. Pud hadn't been able to find anything for her so I got her a lovely brooch and earrings.

19
SUNDAY

Gordon at the Gang Show dress rehearsal from quarter
to 3 to twenty past 10! Shirley was furious! Made a
postbox for the form.

20
MONDAY

The staff gave a wizard concert this afternoon. Talk
about laugh – we howled! They did scenes for 1066
at the end, and we just about had hysterics at the get
ups of some! Unforgettable! Went carol singing at the

town hall with school choir – They're having different schools each night. Afterwards we went to see the bells being run in the cathedral – beautiful.

21
TUESDAY

Never a minute all morning – dashing around all over the place. Said my poem in The Nativity Service & the UIVths were most impressed! Got a card signed by about 6 LVths, whom I've never heard of "With love" – soppy things. I'll soon de-crush them & all the rest I hear about. My report was wizard – really glowing. Super day.

22
WEDNESDAY

Well, started at the laundry! We arrived there at 7.45, & had to wait until 8.30 for Mr Batson. It was most peculiar, cycling down in the dark. I am on packing parcels, Pat & Joyce are on racking. The work is okay, but there is the most beastly overseer (you couldnt call her a supervisor) called Miss Gibson. The two tea breaks at 9.30 and 3.30, music-while-you work, & carol records are the high spots of the day! Jolly tired. The dash home for dinner was pretty grim, too.

23
THURSDAY

Managed to get up okay – it was beastly going out into the cold though, & there was half a gale blowing. The tea break was luscious! It fairly bucks you up. Made quite a few mistakes today – I had half the factory scatty! The girls are all very nice to me – rough & ready types, not very intelligent, but kind and helpful.

24
FRIDAY

Finished work at 12.30 today – whoopee! Had time to stop and talk to M. on my way home from work. Got 19 measly shillings for 2 days – daylight robbery! Pud & I went to the "Gang Show" at the theatre and enjoyed it very much indeed – what they lacked in quality they made up for in enthusiasm.

25
SATURDAY

A. Jean and U. Dave arrived to spend Xmas day with us. We had a whizzing dinner – turkey was scrummy. Got some nice presents, but Mum got piles more – she deserves them, shes so kind & good. Went to Mrs. Gillespies later (!). Late home.

26
SUNDAY

Went to church with Gordon & Pud – sang same carols as yesterday. A & U departed after dinner. Had a bubble bath but it didn't work!

27
MONDAY

Helped round house in the morning (after a late rise!) Helped mum prepare the tea for ten – the Gillespies, us, Shirley & Jennifer. It was super, too. We had quite a good party – but Pud, of course bungled all the games & tricks (trust her, the nincompoop!) It gave us a good laugh though!

28
TUESDAY

Back to work again – I say that like a veteran! Work

just the same, the same dreary monotony of packing parcel after parcel, all the same almost. Dad was still off and he took Mum & Pud to see "The High & The Mighty" at the Lonsdale. Went to bed at 7.30, and read "Wuthering Heights" until nearly ten. Wish it was a fortnight today.

29
WEDNESDAY

We were all tired at work today. The tea break was most welcome, you can bet your last dime! It must be awful working in a factory all your life – it would drive me to suicide, honestly. Those hardened old hags of supervisors are more to be pitied than disliked. I'm getting along fine with my "workmates". Gwen is a scream – I cant stop laughing at her! Mary Mott (Killing name!) is only fifteen & swears like a trooper.

The language of some of them is to be wondered at.

30
THURSDAY

Colder than usual this morning – so the ride down to the laundry was pretty grim. Mucked up clocking in at dinnertime – did Joyces instead of mine & then she did her own when she came because I'd put it back in the "out" slot – so had some explaining to do to "Our Les"! He took it in, for him, a good humour! Had a good chat to Lorna on way home.

31
FRIDAY

Finished at the laundry at 3.30 – Pat & Joyce finished at three, as they were in the first half of the factory.

I was in the very last – the packing. Mum & Dad
went off this evening to Uncle Daves and Aunty Jeans
Silver Wedding celebrations. Joan came to stay the
weekend with Pud – what a pair! Washed the mop &
had a bath as well!

1 JANUARY
SATURDAY

Gordon & I stayed in bed all morning while Pud &
Joan amused themselves making the dinner – & it
was good, too! Went for a walk in the afternoon then
read. Shirley came up for her tea. Joan & I listened to
"Late Love" – Super!

2
SUNDAY

Didn't go to church – stayed at home and did the
housework.

Books Read.   January.

1. MUSICAL HONOURS - Kitty Barne. Nothing special.
2. STRANGE CONFLICT — Dennis Wheatley. Super as per usual
3. WHITE BOOTS - NOEL STREATFEILD. Babyish but enjoyable
4. The BODY IN BEDFORD SQUARE - D. Fume. Not very good.
5. Barry gets his wish. S. Tring - passable but not exceptional
6. Worrals carries on — Not bad.
7. TENNIS SHOES. Noel Streatfeild - VG really.
        No of books read = 7   Best = "Strange Conflict"

        7.

        FEBUARY

1. We didn't mean to go to sea - A. Ransome. Good.
2. Death in the Rising Sun - J. Creasey — Very Good.
3. Crazy Castle — David Severn___ Jolly amusing.
        Exams ∴ didn't have much time hence
        low number of g.
        Best: "DEATH IN THE RISING SUN".

        3.

        MARCH

1. Secret in the Sand - M.E— — Fairly good.
2. THE VILLAGE — Marghanita Laski - VG. Typical.
3. Seven times Seven - J. Creasey - Smashing.
4. Cabin for Crusoe — D. Severn —Fairly Good.
5. Jane Eyre - Charlotte Brontë — an exciting story. A
   modern novelist could make a hit from it. Enjoyed it
much more than when I was 10, when I loathed it.
6. Reach for the sky - Spitting- Paul Brickhill.
7. Garden of God - Stacpoole - interesting.
8. Autumn Term - Antonia Forest - Very good.
        8.   Best = REACH FOR THE SKY.

APRIL

1. Windoms Way - J. Ullman - Average interest
2. Caravan for Five - Not bad - D. Severn.
3. Rainbow Valley - Montgomery - Moderately readable; bit stale then
4. Pollyanna of Magic Valley - Moffit - Pleasant story.
5. Traitors Doom - J. Creasey - V.G. Exciting.
6. *Campbells Kingdom - Innes - V.G. Very Good Story & worth it
7. The 5 sons of Le Faber - Raymond - Quite good
8. The Devil Rides Out - Dennis Wheatley - VG.
9. The cockhouse at Fellsgarth - Reed - Amusing in places

MAY

1. Card goes on the Stage, — Helen Dores-- — Good story.
2. Card in Rep. — ·· .. — J. enjoyable.
3. Holiday exchange — Fairly good.
3.4 By Special Request - ed. Noel Streatfield - VG.
4.5 Kennel Maid Nan — Brent Pyer - Bit Technical.

        No really outstanding this month. No. 3 was very
        good but can hardly be counted as one story.

JUNE

1. Curtain of Fear - Dennis Wheatley — VG indeed.
2. Schoolgirl for Pluck — Coatts — Putrid, lousy, awful.
3. Chentfield School Mystery - M. Marsden - Good [& Readable].
4. Operation Conquest - Gray — Super.
5. Toffy - B. Smith - Amusing.
6. Rachael changes schools — Quite a good story
7. Simon - Sutcliffe - Gd.

JULY

1. Doomsday Men - Priestly - Good.
2. Trouble!- Graeme - Good but muddled.
3. Men on a Donkey - Prescott - Good.
4. Mary Tudor - Prescott - Boring.

AUGUST

1. Jane Eyre - liked it much better but still cant
   say 9 date on it.

<u>NB</u> resolved to give my eyes a rest & so didn't
   read any books.

SEPTEMBER

1. Young Bess - very good - Irwin
2. Elizabeth, Captive Princess - good - Irwin.
3. Dickon - very good.

   NB Work was so much that I
      just hadnt time to read anything
      except background stuff for thropey,
      but enjoyed these three very much

OCTOBER

1. Bleak House - Dickens - very good.
2. They lived: A Brontë novel - good but superficial
3. Life of Charlotte Brontë - Mrs. Gaskell - not bad at all.
4. Wolsey - Pollard - stinking.
5. Thomas More - Potter - very good.
6. The Old Curiosity Shop - jolly good - Dickens.

NOVEMBER

1. Flush - Virginia Woolf - a very good little story.
2. Orlando - Virginia Woolf - No comment!
3. Biggles gets his men - Jolly good light relief! - Johns.
4. Charles V - very heavy! - Karl Brandi
6. Doctor in the house - Gordon - Jolly good.
7. The sword of fate - wheatley - not so good as usual
8. The English Reformation - Parker - not bad at all.

DECEMBER.

1. Margaret of Austria - UB. - Jane de Iongh.
2. The Monday Story - James Legoor - quite good.
3. Wuthering Heights - E. Brontë - very good, re-read.
4. Villette - C. Brontë - G/W. Slow but deep.
5. The Shropshire Lad - Houseman - wonderful.

———

No. BOOKS READ IN YEAR = 66
    AVERAGE   = a. 1 a week or
                        5 a month.

BEST BOOKS OF THE YEAR.
"WUTHERING HEIGHTS"
"MARGARET OF AUSTRIA"
"REACH FOR THE SKY"
"DICKON"

FAVOURITE AUTHORS
Paul Brickhill   Dennis Wheatley
John Creasey   Margaret Irwin.

Pictures seen in 1954. & Comments.

The Intruder.	VG. Jack Hawkins is very clever.
Dobbie Gillis Problem.	G. Light, funny entertainment.
Everest	Marvellous, terrific.
Queens Tour of Fiji	V.G. Colour excellent.
All the brothers were valiant.	Gd. Nice colour but pr. story
The Floating Dutchman.	Quite good.
From here to Eternity.	Good bits. Good on the whole.
Houdini	VG. Good acting. Quick & continuous
Arrowhead	Good colour but story poor.
The Million Pound Note	VG. Very light & amusing.
Two many detectives	Of Average interest
The Kidnappers	VG. Vincent Winter made it.
The last Apache Stand	FG. Nice scenery. Usual story
Doctor in the House.	VG. Very, very funny.
Hobsons Choice	Very Good indeed - esp. John Mills.
Young Bess	Excellent. Esp. J. Simmons & S.G.
Knock on wood	Absolutely daft but V. amusing.
The long, long Trailer	Silly but quite funny.
The Actress	VG.
The Secret Foul	Soppy.
Odette	Marvellous & horrible.
Duel in The Jungle	Scenery & animal shots super.
Fighter Attack	Quite enjoyable.
His majesty O'Keefe	Fair.
The Harassed Hero	Poor
Fixed Bayonets	Very Good.
Racing Blood.	Good.
Genevieve	Nice light amusing film.

{ Late night Final. Authentic S. Land stuff.   G.
{ Elephant Walk. Scenery Superb.   G+

No. of Pictures seen = 19 [sometimes 2 on]

Most Dramatic = "ODETTE"
Funniest   = "DOCTOR IN THE HOUSE"
Most interesting = "THE ASCENT OF EVEREST"
Others worthy of mention:
             HOBSONS CHOICE
             YOUNG BESS
             HOUDINI
             THE KIDNAPPERS

Plays.
1. The love of 4 Colnels - Quite good but nothing startling.   G.
2. The man who came to dinner — Crude —   F.G.
3. The Living Room — moving & disturbing   G+
4. Private Lives - Jolly good, & very amusing.   V.G.
5. Waters of the Moon — Very good & sincere   V.G.
6. One Wild Oat - Coarse - if amusing at times.   F.G.
7. The Deep Blue Sea — Super. Sort I like.   V.G.
8. Home & Beauty - last Act good   G.
9. I lived with you - Jolly amusing   V.G.
10. Dial M for Murder - Super. Smashing plot.   VG indd
11. The Man in Grey — Very good & dramatic.   V.G.
12. Birthday Honours — Very funny   V.G.
13. On the spot - quick but not exceptional.   G.
14. Escapade; Very good & funny too at times   G.
15. For better, for worse - Very funny but wizard   V.G.
16. The burning glass - Jolly dramatic   V.G.
17. The Little Hut - Very obscene but funny!   V.G.

18. Someone Waiting. Pace bit slow.   V.G.
19. A Question of Fact. Bit slow.   G.
20. The Happy Marriage. Rather silly.   G.

Many of these plays were too crude, vulgar & coarse for enjoyment, but there were some really good, clean comedies & also some excellent thrillers.

Best Comedy: Private Lives
                Birthday Honours.
Best thriller: Dial M. for Murder
Best of others: The Deep Blue Sea

Of the rep. company Richard Hart showed great promise & I bet, with a bit of luck, he'll climb higher. Brenda Saunders had a flair for character studies & if she sticks to comedy parts she'd do better.

Best actresses: JEAN SIMONS
                 ADRIENNE CORRI
                 [also chief woman in "Hobsons choice"]
Best Actors: * STEWART GRANGER
               KENNETH MOORE
               TONY CURTIS
               DANNY KAYE
        * JOHN MILLS

Dr.   Cr.

		£	s	d				£	s	d
	Xmas money	4	10	0						
					Dress			2	10	0
					Jeans [I H]			2	0	0
		4	1	0						
Jan 1	Pkt Money		2	6	Pictures				2	6
			1	6	Saved				1	6
					Spent on School things					
Jan 8	Pkt money		2	6	Lime				2	6
			1	6	Saved				3	6
	Extra.		2	0						
Jan 15	Pkt money		3	0	Saved				3	0
Jan 22	.. ..		4	6				−		6
								+ 4	6	
					B3			5	0	
Jan 29	.. ..		4	6	Saved			4	6	

MONTHLY TOTAL :

		£	s	d
Total amt received	=	1	2	0
Spent	=		11	6
Saved			10	6

M. Foster

Dr.   Cr.

	Cash in hand from Jan.		10	6
Feb.5	Waspic.		2	6
	Exam Equip.		2	6
	Left. ✓		5	6
Feb.5.	Pocket money.	4 0	✓ 1	0
	+		4	0
	Mums present		5	0
	card			6d
	Left		4	0
Feb 7th	Beans money		1	6
			5	6
Feb 12	Pkt money		34	0
	Beans		1	6
			10	0
	Card for M. Grenfell — Mum paid			
Feb 19	Pkt money		8	0
	Beans		1	6
			14	6.
	2/- from A.J spent on Flico +		1	6
			13	0
	Petersham		1	4
			11	8
Feb 26	Pkt money		8	0
	Beans		1	6
			16	2
	Monthly Total:	£	s	d
	Received:	1	1	0
	+ from Jan Spent:		10	6
	Spent:		15	4
	Saved		16	2

M. Forster

Dr.   Cr.

Date	Source	Sum £ s d	Spent	Amount £ s d
	Cash in hand from last Feb.			16 2
				16 2
			Comb	5
				15 9
Mar 5	Pkt money	3 0		4 6
	Bean	1 6		
		4 6		20 3
Mar 12	Pkt money	3 0		
	Bean	1 6		
		4 6		
	Pat from M. Peildun	6		5 0
		5 0		25 3
			Blouse	25 3
			Owe	2 8
	Godens Birthday present			5 0
	{taken from Jean money}		Owe	7 8
Mar 19	Pkt money	3 0	[Paid back Mar. 26]	
	Bean	1 6	Cancelled	2 8 some
		4 6	Put back	1 10
			Still owed	3 2
Mar 26	Pkt money	3 0		
	Bean.	1 6	Tights &	2 0
		4 6	dye	2 6
			Still owed	0. 8d
	M. Forster		Recieved.	18 6
			Spent	19 2
			Owed	8.

Dr.   2/6 flow.   **Cr.**

	Owed			8	2/6 A. 5 spent Smartie
	L V¹ concert			6	Magazine Book Club
			1	2	2/6 Aunty Elk.
Apr. 2	Pkt money		2	6	= 3 6.
	Bran.		1	6	Bran = 1 0
			4	0	4s 6d + 4 6
		−	1	2	= 9 0
			3	10.	School things 4 3½
	Magazine			6	4 8½
			3	4	Mag. 4½
	Pru. Pattinson		1	0	4 4
			2	4	6 6
	V¹ concert			4	10 6
			2	0	
	SPECIAL				
	Easter present from	1	0	0	Gave to mum towards
	Gran & A. Nano		10	0	my blazer.
	Uncle Lens Easter	1	10	0	
	Present =		10	0	
April 9-11th Gran & Dado		4	6	= 6 6
					Pictures 3 6
					Cream cakes 1 0
					4 6
			2	0	− 8·0 for book club
April 16	Dado pocket money		5	0	left Flowers + 4 0
		SPENT 1	0	money towards 1 0
	21- from Bean, 21- from Gr & David				picture + E.S.
	gave for petrol.				collection
April 23	Granda & D.		4	6	
April 30	Granda & D.		6	6	M. Foster

Dr.   Cr.

	Pm April	10	10	SPECIAL: Jeans 2	0 0
	Woman T Coller.		8	U.L.	10 2
		10	2	Dress coto Pud	1 5 0
May 7.	Pads & Brand.	4	6	Total: £3	5 0
		14	8	— Jeans 1	18 6
	Hazels card & Derby bet	1	8	3	9 6
	Mag.	13	0	5	8 0
May 14	Pads & Beans	4	6	= — £4	2 6
		17	6	5	8 0
				Owe Mum £1	5 6
				Gill 5/- Birth £1	0 6
May 21st	Pad & Bran			Theatre, Pud.	4 6
				1	5 0
	Birthday Presents	10	0	Mum	
		5	0	Dad	
		10	0	Gordon	
		10	0	A. Jean	
		10	0	A. Nan	
		1 10	0	Branda.	
		7	6	Ellen & Shirley (5/-)	
	Mum wouldn't take debt	1 5	0		
		5 7	6		
	Theatre	3	6		
		5 4	0		
	Cardigan	1 0	0		
	Pyjamas + slip	1 0	0		
		3 4	0		
	S.C. Things	4	0		
		3 0	0		

<u>NB</u> AT THIS POINT, FOUND had only £2 7.6d in Kitty — so could not find it & gave up in despair, hence did not record spendings until after bought Pyjamas ———→

Dr.   Cr.

		£	s	d			
		1	12	0			
Junell Bran & Dad			4	6			
		1	16	6			
Give up!				1			

	JAN.	FEB.	MAR.	APR.	MAY	JUNE	JULY	AUG.	SEPT.	OCT.	NOV.	DEC.

Xmas Presents.

Money

	£	s	d	
Granda	2	0	0	used bef. xmas
A. Jean		10	0	used bef x.
A. Nan		10	0	used bef x.
U. Len.		10	0	used bef x.
A. Sally		5	0	
Mrs. B.		5	0	
Mrs. Car.		2	6	
M. Reid.		5	0	used for x. pres.
Dad		10	0	used b. x.
	£0	12	6	

Other

Gordon	Sliperettes
Pud	Mits & Scarf
Mum	Slip
Dad	Silk Red. Belt
Jean Boyd & Co.	Book
Mary Baines	Soaps & etc.
M.	Solid Eau de Col.

MARGARET FORSTER was the author of many successful and acclaimed novels, including *Have the Men Had Enough?*, *Lady's Maid*, *Diary of an Ordinary Woman*, *Is There Anything You Want?*, *Keeping the World Away*, *Over* and *The Unknown Bridesmaid*. She also wrote bestselling memoirs – *Hidden Lives*, *Precious Lives* and, most recently, *My Life in Houses* – and biographies of Daphne du Maurier and Elizabeth Barrett Browning. She was married to writer and journalist Hunter Davies and lived in London and the Lake District. She died in February 2016, just before her last novel, *How to Measure a Cow*, was published.